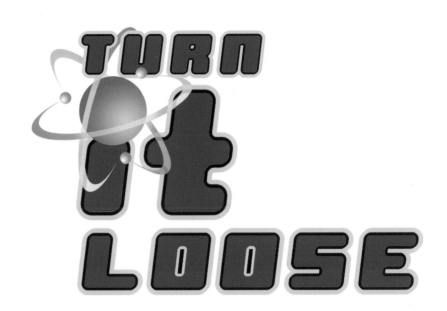

TURN it LOOSE

By **Diane Swanson**

Illustrations by **Warren Clark**

The Scientist in **ABSOLUTELY** Everybody

ANNICK PRESS

TORONTO + NEW YORK + VANCOUVER

Annick Press Ltd.

We acknowledge the support of the Canada Council for the Arts, the Ontario Arts Council, and the Government of Canada through the Book Publishing Industry Development Program (BPIDP) for our publishing activities.

Editing by Pam Robertson
Copy editing by Elizabeth McLean
Cover design by Irvin Cheung/iCheung Design
Interior design by Warren Clark

Cataloging in Publication

Swanson, Diane, 1944–
    Turn it loose : the scientist in absolutely everybody / by Diane Swanson;
    illustrated by Warren Clark.

    Includes bibliographical references and index.
    ISBN 1-55037-851-1 (bound).—ISBN 1-55037-850-3 (pbk.)

    1. Science—Juvenile literature. 2. Science—Methodology—Juvenile
literature. I. Clark, Warren II. Title.
Q163.S93 2004   j500   C2003-906008-X

The text was typeset in Frutiger 45 light
Printed and bound in Belgium

Published in the U.S.A. by	**Distributed in Canada by**	**Distributed in the U.S.A. by**
by Annick Press (U.S.) Ltd	Firefly Books Ltd.	Firefly Books (U.S.) Inc.
	66 Leek Crescent	P.O. Box 1338
	Richmond Hill, ON	Ellicott Station
	L4B 1H1	Buffalo, NY 14205

Visit our website at www.annickpress.com

Dedication

For Jeffrey, Justin, and Malachy,
young scientists exploring this fascinating world

Acknowledgments

Heartfelt thanks go to Pam Robertson whose editing skills
are ever clever and gracious, Warren Clark whose genius
in illustration and design makes my words look good,
Elizabeth McLean whose copy-editing is always sharp-eyed
and thorough, Irvin Cheung whose inventive concept gave
this publication an amazing face, the super gang at Annick
Press whose creative and steadfast support is enormously
appreciated, and the many people whose thinking and
writing inspired this work—especially philosophers Lee Nisbet
and Susan Haack; scientists Richard Dawkins, Carl Sagan,
Richard Feynman, C.P. Snow, Edith Cobbs, and Rachel Carson;
and educators Bess-Gene Holt and Ronald Weeks.

Contents

The Scientist in YOU

As a person, you're a combo—a unique combination of interests, knowledge, talents, and skills.

YOU MAY BE A SKATEBOARDER, SINGER, SWIMMER, CHESS CHAMP, CLASS CLOWN, DIRT BIKER, ARTIST, MODEL CAR BUILDER, SOCCER PLAYER, SAXOPHONIST, SKIER, PET OWNER, MOVIE BUFF, AUTOGRAPH HOUND, TRACK SPRINTER, STAMP COLLECTOR, JAZZ DANCER, VIDEO GAME EXPERT— EVEN ALL OF THESE.

But whatever or whoever you are, you are also a scientist.

Yes, YOU.

There's a scientist in absolutely everybody. Not a trained, professional one, of course, but a natural, inborn scientist. It's been with you since you were a baby. It guided your first observations—that all those fingers at the ends of your arms were actually parts of you and that the two feet in your crib belonged to you, too.

By experimenting—simple trial and error stuff—you found out where your mouth was and discovered how to stick things into it. Then you made more observations by tasting: a strand from the rug (yucky), your own toes (not bad), chunks of melon (sweet). Bit by bit—or bite by bite—you learned what you liked to put into your mouth and what you didn't.

As you started to crawl, you expanded your scientific explorations. You found you could slide more easily across a wooden floor than a carpet. You could peek through windows, but not through walls. When you pulled open a cupboard door, you could slam it shut and make a loud BANG. Every time. The discoveries have never stopped.

Having a scientist inside meant you were a curious person with ways of following up your interests and putting together your world. It's what made you keen to wonder, question, imagine, investigate, observe, compare, guess, experiment, and figure things out. After all, science is mostly a style of thinking—not a pile of facts.

> "Science is the story we tell ourselves...to make sense of the world."
> —Sue Halpern, science writer

You may not realize it, but your inner scientist still influences much of what you do today. It's the part of you that automatically observes the direction a ball is moving, estimates its speed, and figures out where you need to be to catch it—all in an instant. Your scientific self helps you sing by comparing different sounds and the relationships between them. You can easily pick out notes that are eight apart—like two Cs or two As—because the higher-pitched note vibrates twice as fast as the lower one. Even if you don't *know* that, your ear hears it. Your brain compares and records the sounds and the relationships—naturally.

Of course, just because you *think* like a scientist doesn't mean that you want to *be* a scientist. Scientific thinking is part of everyone's life. Always has been. When German composer Ludwig van Beethoven was busy writing his *Moonlight Sonata* in 1801, he was **connecting** sounds and **locating patterns** of harmony and rhythm. The third president of the United States, Thomas Jefferson, thought of himself as a scientist and drew on his abilities to **question, investigate**, and **compare** to guide his leadership and promote democracy. And all athletes—Olympic or amateur—**observe** and **analyze** the competitions they're in and **figure out** how to improve their skills.

> "I go where the puck is going, not where it was."
> —Wayne Gretzky, hockey professional

Even though everyone has an inner scientist, people don't all think the same way. Like everybody else, you are an individual with a style that's your own. You might investigate a situation by asking a lot of questions, or you might prefer to watch, explore, and discover. People even observe things differently. Some depend mostly on what they see; others need to touch and feel. What one person tunes in, another may tune out, but everybody develops a method of scientific thinking that works for him or her. Experience helps mold that style.

LIKE *a Pro*

The thinking that goes on inside you is a lot like the thinking that happens in the heads of professional scientists. You ask questions, they ask questions. You observe, they observe. You compare, they compare. And so on. But through years and years of hard work, professional scientists have honed their scientific minds. They've become trained think-tanks, able to set up complex experiments and solve difficult problems in their fields. It's their job to use science to find out how things work. Exactly how do viruses spread? What makes those sounds that come from outer space? How far do hummingbirds fly when they migrate?

The difference between professional scientists and you is a little like the difference between professional drummers and you. It takes loads and loads of training and practice to beat the drums as well as the pros, but, by drawing on your own ability to hear rhythms, you can appreciate their performances.

Still, inside every professional scientist, an inborn scientist lives on. Take Jean Henri Fabre. Born in France in 1823, he was an outdoor explorer from the time he could walk, and he was brimming with curiosity about beetles, butterflies, rocks, and water.

When he was five, he wondered, "Do I see with my mouth or my eyes?" And he did a science experiment to find out. Facing the sun, he shut his eyes tightly and opened his mouth. Then he shut his mouth tightly and opened his eyes. He repeated the experiment over and over before making any conclusions.

Always poor, Jean learned mostly on his own—even when doing the research that finally earned him a Doctor of Science degree. And after he became a professional scientist, he continued to draw on his inborn scientist to help him study insects. Like the child he once was, Jean followed wasps and bees to their nests. He figured out how long it took burial beetles to bury a dead mole. He noticed what a praying mantis ate and how it captured its meals. English naturalist Charles Darwin called him an "incomparable observer."

Not only did Jean rely on his own inborn scientist, he also called on the scientists inside his children. Their keen perception and intense curiosity helped him find specimens and make observations. When his son, Paul, was only seven, he was an authority on insects such as dung beetles and crickets. And Jean recalled Paul's thrill the night the boy discovered 40 great peacock moths flocking to a female that had emerged from her cocoon in a cage: "Little Paul, half-undressed, is rushing about, jumping and stamping, knocking the chairs over like a mad thing. I hear him call me: 'Come quick!' he screams. 'Come and see these moths, big as birds! The room is full of them!'"

Drawing on the scientists inside his children and himself—as well as on his professional scientific self—helped Jean Henri Fabre become France's greatest naturalist and one of the top investigators of insect behavior.

> "The whole of science is nothing more than a refinement of everyday thinking."
> —Albert Einstein, physicist

TURN IT *Loose*

Lucky for you that you think like a scientist. It helps you develop your mind, learn to reason, and understand the world around you. As you grow up, it will help you do better at whatever you choose to do—play tennis, raise a family, solve crimes, construct buildings, study the stars, paint pictures, drive a semi, teach school, run a business, design software, sail a boat, practice medicine, lead a country, or simply enjoy nature.

The trouble is that it's possible for you to fall out of touch with your inborn scientist. That curious, investigative, full-of-wonder part of you can wither and fade if you ignore it. Just as you wouldn't dream of starving your body of exercise until you were too weak to lift this book, don't let your amazing scientific self slip away. The "use it or lose it" slogan applies as much to your inner scientist as it does to any of the muscles in your body.

Keeping your inner scientist alive and well isn't hard. All you have to do is turn it loose in your everyday life. That means feeling free to do the things your inborn scientist has always been eager to do:

- let your mind overflow with wonder,
- ask questions—always,
- think for yourself,
- set your imagination soaring,
- investigate: search for facts,
- persist, persist, persist,
- collect whatever's neat—and classify it, too,
- observe the world around you,
- record special observations,
- compare what you observe,
- make connections,
- spot patterns,
- design or plan stuff,
- take a guess,
- make mistakes (they're so revealing!),
- hang in there—be patient,
- experiment: see for yourself,
- measure stuff,
- figure out answers,
- see the inconsistencies,
- analyze—break things down,
- share your discoveries: communicate, and
- use the scientific method.

The chapters in this book discuss all these scientific actions and tell stories about real people who made them important in their lives—from childhood on. By exercising their inner scientists, they found it easier to do what mattered to them. Some of them grew up to be scientists. Others became astronauts, pilots, naturalists, inventors, fossil collectors, mathematicians, and program designers. Still others—and they may surprise you—became artists, musicians, politicians, writers, volunteer workers, and sports professionals. They, too, used scientific thinking to excel in their fields.

All of these people became famous for their work. Perhaps their stories will inspire you to achieve great things. By exercising your inner scientist, you can do what is important to you. And that's what counts.

At the end of each of the following chapters, you'll see a section called "Brainplay." It suggests ways to keep your inborn scientist strong and fit—while having fun. And because scientific heads like yours have creative minds, each Brainplay will make you think of variations or more activities that can turn your inner scientist loose.

So go for it!

Look to the Stars

Tell Flash Gordon to move over. Okay, so he's a brave Earthling. He overthrew the evil Ming the Merciless, self-proclaimed emperor of the universe. He freed the enslaved inhabitants of Planet Mongo. Big deal. He exists only in comics and movies, unlike flesh-and-blood Roberta.

Armed with a water pistol—just like Flash Gordon's—the eight-year-old set out to explore a *real* planet: Earth. Well, a section of it, anyway—her neighborhood. Roberta's sister, Barbara, also armed with a water pistol, went with her. It was 1953, and they were wearing the new space helmets they'd ordered from the people at Dubble Bubble Gum.

When the helmets had first arrived in the mail, they had been a bit disappointing. They were made only of cardboard, nothing like the girls had expected. But assembled, the tall helmets looked good, even professional. The girls popped them on and peered out through the wide openings. They felt well prepared for their next "mission" and headed off to their plywood spacecraft.

Whenever Roberta and Barbara traveled beyond Earth (their yard) to explore imaginary planets or asteroids, they searched for signs of life: plants, animals, and humanoids (neighbors and delivery people were probably never aware of the roles they played in these make-believe space dramas).

"Click!" went Roberta's Brownie camera each time she spotted some strange life-form. She had decided it was important to keep a careful report of her findings.

On camping trips and weekend journeys along nearby Lake Superior, Roberta felt the pull of the universe even more. Away from the bright lights of her hometown, she could see the planets and stars more clearly. They seemed to call to her. Nothing, but nothing, held as much wonder for Roberta as the idea of exploring the skies. "I spent all my free time dreaming about space," she admitted later, as an adult.

That sense of wonder bolstered Roberta Bondar through many long years of study at universities. It also helped her learn to fly a plane. And in 1983, she was chosen from among thousands of other applicants to be trained as an astronaut. Her Dubble Bubble space helmet was going to be replaced by the real thing. By January 1992, Roberta was making her childhood dreams come true—soaring through the universe on the space shuttle *Discovery*!

LET YOUR MIND OVERFLOW WITH *Wonder*

If Roberta had never looked skyward, filled with wonder about the mysteries of the universe, she would have remained an Earth-bound creature. Her space travel would have been restricted to taking imaginary rides on rocket ships in Flash Gordon comic strips. For sure, she followed up her wondering with hard work, but her dreams of exploring the skies as an astronaut kept her going.

Wondering is an important part of the nature of any scientist. Imagine the sense of wonder that must lead researchers in submersibles to explore vents at the bottom of the Pacific and Atlantic oceans. Spewing scalding water, some of these deep-sea vents build up towering chimneys from the minerals that settle out, and they are home to ghostly white crabs, giant clams, and other life seen nowhere else. And think of the curiosity that propels scientists to investigate 500-million-year-old fossils of bizarre creatures found high in the Rocky Mountains. The Burgess Shale—as the spot is called—is rich with the remains of more than 100 different species, including some of the world's most perfectly preserved fossils. Wonder excites scientists to discover what swam or roamed Earth in the distant past.

"Wisdom begins in wonder."
—Socrates, philosopher

So what fills you with wonder? Makes you shiver in awe? As a toddler, you might have been amazed by the cool tingling of snowflakes landing on your nose or the feathered flurry of ducks rising suddenly from a pond. Today, it might be tales of gigantic dinosaurs that capture your excitement. But whatever sets you off, it's your sense of wonder that makes you eager to learn more.

Poked and prodded by the mysteries of what's there and what's yet to come, your wonder at everything from an ordinary earthworm to the planet Mars soars and thrives. It creates a powerful drive for you to know and understand, and more than anything else, it keeps your mind sharp.

BRAINPLAY

⭐ Wonder begins with what you sense. Give your senses—and your wonder—a workout:

- Look for a trail of silvery slime left by a slug, and wonder how it helps slugs travel up the side of a fence and how it protects their soft bodies.
- Smell flowers at noon, then again after dark, and wonder why some smell stronger at night.
- Listen to a fly zoom past, and wonder how it makes the sounds you hear.
- Taste a slice of a fresh lemon, and wonder what makes it so sour.
- Touch one of the threads that anchors a spider's web to a bush. Then touch a thread close to the center of the web, and wonder why one thread is sticky while the other is not.

Follow up each of your wonderings by checking books or the Internet for more information.

⭐ Place a penny on your palm, and picture the travels it might have taken...the pockets it might have visited. Picture where it might go and how it could change if you dropped it into a stream.

⭐ Ever wonder if you could grow the seeds in the oranges you eat? Find out. Rinse off a few fat seeds, then soak them in water for 24 hours. Put potting soil in little pots with holes in the bottom for drainage. Plant the seeds—one per pot—beneath 1 centimeter (1/2 inch) of moist soil, and cover them with paper towels. Stand the pots in a warm spot, and keep the soil moist.

Each day, peek under the towels. When the seeds sprout green shoots, remove the towels and stand the pots in indirect light. After a week, move them to direct light.

⭐ Think of one of your favorite things...your pet cat...a picnic at the beach...flashes of lightning...pop music...and wonder what you would do if you knew you could never experience it again.

Why, Why, Why?

"I remember the streets made a maze, filthy with foul garbage. We were very poor, taking lodging in rooms over a coach house," said Michael. When he was a boy in England during the 1790s, his large family (he had nine brothers and sisters!) rarely had enough to eat. "For a time, my mother could give me little more than a loaf of bread a week," he said.

But Michael's mind was as rich as he was poor. He was bursting with curiosity, asking streams of questions, even while helping his father at work in the blacksmith's shop. Why does fire burn so hot? How does it bend metal? Why do horses need shoes?

When Michael was 13, he had to leave school and get a job to support himself. He worked first as an errand boy, but soon got a chance to train as a bookbinder. It was the perfect job for him. He read nearly all the books he bound—especially the ones about science—and found answers to questions that kept popping into his head. How do clocks keep time? What makes a telescope work? Why do things fall down, not up?

One day, Michael was binding a volume of the *Encyclopedia Britannica* and discovered an article on electricity that described a few experiments. Spellbound, he wanted to try them out himself, and he did—as soon as he could afford to buy some simple equipment. Doing his first set of experiments helped him answer some questions he had about electricity—but it also raised more.

> "I badgered my parents constantly with questions. Where did color come from? What happened to the sugar when one stirred it into the tea? Why did water bubble when it boiled?"
> —Oliver Sacks, doctor and author

When he was a young man, Michael managed to get work that was closer to the science he loved. It was only a job washing bottles, but it was at the Royal Institution, a center for science research and teaching in London. He took his curiosity to work with him every day, and before long, he was allowed to experiment in the basement labs on his own time. There, his questioning mind bubbled over. Just how does electricity work? Is it possible to generate electricity through magnetism?

By asking questions and searching for answers, Michael Faraday managed to give himself an amazing education. Eventually, he became a leading scientist, especially in the field of electricity. He was the first to show that magnetism can be used to produce electric currents.

BRAINPLAY

⭐ English author Rudyard Kipling (1865–1936) wrote a short poem about the importance of asking questions:
"I keep six honest serving men
They taught me all I knew:
Their names are What and Why and When
And How and Where and Who."

Look all around you. When something grabs your attention, find out everything you can about it. Use the Kipling questions as a guide.

⭐ Pretend you're a newspaper reporter working the crime beat. List some of the questions you would ask each of these people:
- a baker arrested for selling poisoned pies,
- the police officer who arrested the baker, and
- the baker's helper.

⭐ Question absolutely everything—even stories of superheroes. If you just assume they're complete fantasies, you'll miss out on the chance to ask some super questions—and find some neat information. In a class called "Everything I Know of Science I Learned from Reading Comic Books," physics professor Jim Kakalios of Minnesota asks questions such as, "Would Spiderman's silk really be strong enough to carry him from building to building?"

Ask Questions... ALWAYS

Michael Faraday's ever questioning mind led to discoveries that enriched the entire world. You can thank him for making electric machinery possible—even the portable stereo and headset that let you listen to your favorite music as you walk to school.

Scientists are extraordinarily curious. No matter what their field, they tend to run wild with questions. Is there other intelligent life in the universe? Just how does gravity operate? What makes deep-sea sharks rise to shallow water? Questions help scientists focus their research and spur them to hunt for answers. After all, experimenting is a way of asking and answering questions.

It's natural—and useful—for everybody to ask questions. Every day, you probably ask more than you realize. Besides the practical stuff—"Where's the glue?" or "Are

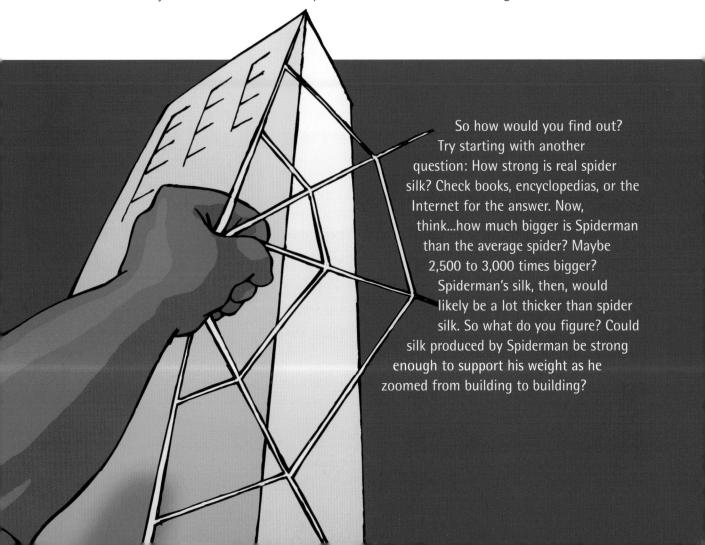

So how would you find out? Try starting with another question: How strong is real spider silk? Check books, encyclopedias, or the Internet for the answer. Now, think...how much bigger is Spiderman than the average spider? Maybe 2,500 to 3,000 times bigger? Spiderman's silk, then, would likely be a lot thicker than spider silk. So what do you figure? Could silk produced by Spiderman be strong enough to support his weight as he zoomed from building to building?

we out of juice?"—your mind brims with questions ranging from "How come Justin's bike goes faster uphill than mine?" to "What makes the air so muggy?"

British author Roger Highfield even questioned the fantasy life he read about in Harry Potter novels. He contacted more than 100 scientists to see if any of the wild and crazy things in Harry's world could possibly be real— things such as the Invisibility Cloak and the Sorting Hat that divided Hogwart's students into four houses. Then Roger used his questions and the answers he received to write a book called, *The Science of Harry Potter: How Magic Really Works.*

One of the most interesting things about questions is that just about every answer leads to another question. Why do squirrels have such sharp claws? To climb trees. Why do they climb trees? That's where they live. How come they live in trees? And so on. Questions keep knowledge advancing. So go right ahead—EXPLODE. Ask every question that pops into your head, then set out to find answers by observing, experimenting, analyzing, reading, and talking to people "in the know." As you read the rest of this book, you'll also discover other ways to search for answers.

Don't worry if some questions go unanswered for a while. Your mind's "antennae" will stay tuned to pick up clues that can help you find answers later, even if you've moved on to thinking about other stuff. The important thing is to keep questioning—it expands your mind. What could be more useful than that?

> **"The important thing is not to stop questioning."**
> —Albert Einstein, physicist

Flying Free

A roller coaster. Maybe that's what got Amelia thinking freely...openly...about what she might do with her life. In 1904, girls didn't have nearly as many opportunities as boys. But that year, seven-year-old Amelia and her family visited the World's Fair in St. Louis, Missouri, and its huge roller coaster inspired her to build one of her own.

Back in Kansas, she ran a rough plank from the roof of a shed to the ground. Then she set a little cart, made of wood and roller skates, at the top and climbed in. But when Amelia tried out her roller coaster, the cart ran off the plank, and she tumbled out. So she tried again, making the ride safer by using a longer plank to create a more gradual slope.

Building a roller coaster was just one of Amelia's "unladylike" activities. She preferred leaping over fences to walking through gates. She collected frogs and worms and watched how they moved. She played football, and sometimes she even went shooting rats with a gun.

During wintertime, Amelia slid down snowy hills on a boy's sled. It offered faster, more thrilling rides than a girl's sled, which was built like a chair on runners for gentle gliding. Once, when the ice was too slippery to stop the sled, she skidded right between the legs of a horse that was hauling a wagon.

An eager reader, Amelia devoured adventures of male characters, such as David Copperfield, Oliver Twist, and the Count of Monte Cristo. She had trouble finding books about plucky girls like her, and she was growing into a determined, independent-minded woman.

The first time Amelia took a ride in an airplane, she decided she wanted to learn to fly one herself. She struggled to earn enough money for lessons, then trained as a pilot. At 24, she made her first solo flight and never looked back.

Soon Amelia Earhart was setting a world record for women, soaring 4,267 kilometers (14,000 feet) above the ground. In 1932, she flew alone, west to east, across the Atlantic Ocean—the first woman ever to do so. And three years later, she became the first person to fly over the Pacific Ocean from Hawaii to California.

Think FOR YOURSELF

If Amelia had done only the things most girls did in the early 1900s, her life would probably have taken a different path. Instead, she thought for herself, following her own interests and keeping alive the independent spirit that later sent her flying across the skies.

Amelia was as much a rebel thinker as Sophie Germain of 18th-century France. Sophie didn't agree with the common belief of the day—that only boys and men needed to use math, so it was unnecessary for girls to learn it. At 13, she began teaching herself math secretly at night, sneaking books into her room and smuggling in candles to read by. Years later, she became a celebrated mathematician.

> **"Where all think alike, no one thinks very much."**
> –Walter Lippmann, author

Thinking independently is important to scientists. They don't trust that something is true or false simply because others say so. They aim to find out for themselves. If Polish astronomer Copernicus (1473–1543) had accepted that the Sun revolved around Earth—which astronomers thought for centuries—he wouldn't have come up with the idea that Earth moved around the Sun. And it's lucky that England's William Harvey (1578–1657) didn't adopt what other doctors of his time believed—that people used up their blood supply, then their bodies made more—or he wouldn't have discovered how blood circulates.

Turn It Loose

You're no sheep. You don't do or think things just because others do. You started becoming an independent person years ago, which is a very good thing. If you had never learned to assert yourself, you wouldn't have followed up your own interests—playing the drums, not the saxophone, or collecting rocks instead of stamps. And if you hadn't become a free thinker, you might still believe folklore that says reindeer can fly.

Of course, an important part of growing up also involves learning from other people, such as parents. But no one wants you to stop thinking for yourself. Now and in the future, you need to be free to consider ideas and events on their own terms—to base your decisions on logic and your opinions on evidence.

BRAINPLAY

⭐ Think independently by challenging the following widely held beliefs. Use recent books and Internet sites to check for information about each one.
- The Great Wall of China is the only human-made structure that is visible from space.
- Most people use only 10 percent of their brain.
- Bats are blind.

⭐ Amelia Earhart was inspired by the independent characters, such as the Count of Monte Cristo, in the books she devoured. Reread a book you love and watch for evidence of characters who think for themselves instead of blindly following the ideas and actions of others. Maybe you've come across a detective who insists on sticking to the evidence to solve a mystery, unlike other characters who jump to conclusions.

⭐ Exercise your ability to think independently. Each of the words in the box is paired with an obvious partner word. Make new, creative partnerships (anything goes!) by linking each "A" word with the two other "B" words, and give a reason why they could connect. For example, you might pair "Salt" with "Saddle" because they both start with "S." What might "Day" and "Saddle" have in common? Ask your friends to do the same exercise and see what they come up with, then create new lists and turn them into a game.

Partner A	Partner B	Reason for Partnership
Salt	Pepper	Same category—spices
Horse	Saddle	Used together
Day	Night	Opposites

Breaking
Through

Imagine being held prisoner by snow—heaps of it. You couldn't go out for food or mail. You couldn't get treatment for injuries or illnesses. In emergencies, even fire trucks couldn't reach you.

That's what life was like during harsh winters in rural Quebec in the early 1900s. No wonder Armand dreamed of driving quickly and easily on top of the snow. He had always had a rich imagination. It's what helped him use junk scavenged from the family farm to create toys, such as the mechanical train engine he made of parts from an old clock.

In 1922, 15-year-old Armand began pulling together ideas for a snow-riding machine. When his family moved to the village of Valcourt, he built the machine secretly inside the garage. His younger brother Leopold helped him find an old farm sleigh and attach the motor and radiator from a wrecked Model T Ford. They also needed an airplane-style propeller—something the boys didn't have—so Armand carved one out of wood. Together, they screwed it to the back of the sleigh.

When it was time to test out the snow-rider, Leopold planted himself firmly at the front. He held tightly onto makeshift reins of cotton rope so he could steer the front runners. Armand switched on the engine, threw open the garage door, and leaped onto the back end. As he shoved the machine into gear, they took off.

From the window, the boys' father barely caught sight of the strange-looking vehicle as it barreled past the house and down Valcourt's snowy main street. But he had no trouble hearing its engine blaring and its propeller spinning wildly. He shot out of the door and chased after the boys.

It took all of Leopold's strength—and then some—to steer the machine while Armand controlled the throttle. Still, they managed to travel more than a kilometer (half a mile) before crashing into a barn. When their father caught up, he was relieved to see that neither of his sons was injured. What's more, Armand was beaming. He had produced one of the very first snowmobiles!

Armand Bombardier soon convinced his father to let him apprentice to become a mechanic, and at age 19 he started his own car repair business. Over the years, he spent time improving his early snowmobile. By 1959, his company was producing a motorcycle-style Ski-Doo on steerable skis. For people in snowbound places, it changed life forever.

SET YOUR IMAGINATION *Soaring*

Think of how Armand's mind broke through the bounds of old thinking. He used his imagination to solve a problem that others had simply tried to live with. By inventing his snowmobile, he delivered people from a wintry prison—and even saved lives by providing a way to get help during emergencies. Today, the Ski-Doo that first took shape in a teenager's imagination is used for everything from rounding up reindeer to driving children to school. It's also widely used as a rescue vehicle on ski hills and as a fun way to explore the snowy outdoors.

> "To invent, you need a good imagination and a pile of junk."
> —Thomas Alva Edison, inventor

Now think of the ways that imagination supports the work of scientists. It expands research possibilities, suggests new directions, and helps solve puzzles. North American ecologist Jeff Goodyear recently figured out how to build a hardy satellite transmitter that could be attached to a wild crocodile. Now there's a challenge to the imagination! A type of rubber acted as a

fast-setting glue to hold the transmitter behind the croc's head so that biologists could track the animal's travels through Venezuela. "We're as much artists as electronic specialists," said Jeff.

You have a busy imagination, too. You dream up new tricks to perform on your bike or skateboard and think of original ways to earn money, perhaps by removing spiders or snakes from your neighbors' homes. Sometimes your imagination takes you on flights of fancy where you picture yourself rescuing people from burning buildings or playing the lead role in a movie.

Imagination can take you far—if you keep it alive. Apply it freely to your own interests and one day, it might have you writing novels, inventing gadgets, teaching

BRAINPLAY

⭐ Do you ever lie on the lawn, spotting clouds shaped like planes, ducks, whatever? Exercise your imagination the same way by finding shapes in doodles. On a blank sheet of paper, make a number of pencil lines: curved and straight, zigzagged and looped. Then look for figures of any kind, turning the paper around in all directions. Use colored pencils to fill in what you see.

Hedge hog

Witch hat

Dinosaur head— mouth open

Bird head

Stealth bomber

school, or solving crimes. Jane (Jenny) Addams's imagination led her to a career in social work. Traveling through an Ohio town with her father, seven-year-old Jane got her first look at poverty...people in houses with broken doors and windows...children in dirty rags, playing in the streets. Shocked, she began to imagine a big house where poor people could get help and children could play. As an adult, Jane's imagination took her to Chicago in 1889 where she found an old mansion in a rundown section of the city. She used the house to provide day care, children's clubs, and education for the needy. She set an example for others who wanted to work with the poor, even helping to establish the National Federation of Settlements and Neighborhood Centers in 1911.

★ Pretend you are a superhero. Picture how you look. Imagine the secret skills you possess. Now sketch yourself in action, saving a friend from the clutches of your archenemy!

★ Listed below are some everyday items with everyday uses. Use your imagination to think of two very different uses for each one. For example, a ruler—normally used to measure things—can be a great back scratcher. Stuck in a pot of soil, it also makes a good support for a plant.
- plastic bowl
- last year's calendar
- egg carton
- funnel
- wire coat hanger

Show your friends the same list and see what their imaginations come up with.

★ Why are manhole covers round, not square? That's a question often asked during interviews at Microsoft Corporation, the American computer software giant. Every month, the company hears from about 12,000 people hunting for jobs. To find the most creative thinkers, Microsoft asks them puzzle questions that call for plenty of imagination.

So why are manhole covers round, not square? Here's a clue: Think about them when they are removed. Imagine which shape of cover, when resting on edge, could accidentally fall into its own hole. Which shape would be easiest to roll along the road?

Tracking It Down

Feed the pigs. Milk the cows. Gather the eggs. Pump the water. The farm chores Rachel did every day helped her discover how nature operated. Sometimes, she also churned the milk, amazed to see the way it thickened and changed into creamy butter. When spring came, she planted a garden, then watered, weeded, and watched it grow. And when fall brought frost to the banks of the Allegheny River, she helped her family harvest fruit and vegetables.

It was 1912, and five-year-old Rachel lived in a hilltop farmhouse outside Pittsburgh, Pennsylvania. When her older brother and sister were off at school, she was left to play alone. Except for Candy, that is. Her faithful dog padded after her everywhere.

As soon as her chores were done, Rachel went exploring. She and Candy roved the fields on the farm. Among the tall grass, they examined scaly skins shed by snakes and fluffy feathers molted by birds. Sometimes they found abandoned nests. And as they splashed through the streams that entered the Allegheny, they watched for fish and hunted for rocks—some rubbed smooth by the moving water.

Before dinner, Rachel often surveyed the woods with her mother—and Candy, of course. Besides watching and listening for birds, they checked out wildflowers and beehives. They traced the buz-z-zing from flower to hive and back again. At night, they scanned the dark sky for constellations—patterns of brilliant stars, such as the Big Dipper and Little Dipper.

As Rachel grew, so did her interest in nature. She studied biology and worked as a scientist and writer, investigating plants and animals. She learned where and how they lived, how they survived and grew, and what killed them. In 1962, she published her discoveries in a book that shook the world. *Silent Spring* told readers how pesticides, such as powerful bug killers, can harm nature. She warned of a spring when there would be no birds left to sing.

The following year, Rachel Carson spoke to the United States Congress, calling for new controls on the use of pesticides...controls that would help protect the environment and human health. Although Rachel died soon after, her investigative work led to the banning of a powerful pesticide called DDT and inspired people everywhere to guard the natural world.

Investigate SEARCH FOR FACTS

When she was a child, Rachel investigated her farm almost daily. No doubt she asked plenty of questions about nature—especially to her mother—but she was also keen to find answers by exploring. Her probing ways later helped her become a nature investigator who made significant discoveries and changed the way people look at the world.

"Discovery consists of seeing what everybody has seen and thinking what nobody has thought."
—Albert Szent-Györgyi, biochemist

Investigating—searching for facts—is part of every scientist's day. Some scientists don't ever leave their labs to investigate. They might pore over microscopes, watching the movements of small insects or tiny, single-celled organisms on glass slides. Other scientists travel the globe to investigate. American geologist Katharine Fowler-Billings hunted for answers to questions that intrigued her as a child, such as how mountains form. For much of the 20th century, her investigations took her through mountain ranges in the United States and as far away as Sierra Leone, in Africa, where she examined their makeup.

Like scientists, you're a natural investigator. You make discoveries by putting your senses to work and asking a lot of questions. You also investigate by checking things out directly—just as Rachel did.

You might skip rocks across the water to find the type and shape that works best or test different kinds of guitar picks to choose the one that makes the cleanest sound.

Keep your investigative skills sharp and years later, you'll still find them useful in all you do— from discovering a great way to invest your savings to locating the best place to train as a DJ.

BRAINPLAY

⭐ Investigate "The Case of the Flying Skateboard." How does a skateboarder do an ollie— make the board fly through the air with its rider—even though it's not strapped on? Find out by gathering the facts of the case. Note:
- the shape of the skateboard,
- the position of the feet as the skateboarder starts a jump,
- the action of the back foot as the skateboarder jumps, and
- the position of the feet when the skateboarder is airborne.

Watch skateboarders do several ollies. Can you figure out what's happening? Check your conclusions by asking skateboarders how they do ollies.

⭐ Investigate "The Case of the Front, Back, Up, and Down Worm." You've seen plenty of earthworms, but can you tell their front ends from their back, or their tops from their bottoms? Find out by investigating a worm.

Dark days are best for unearthing worms because they tend to avoid light. Dig in damp soil beneath a rock, dump the soil to one side, then move your fingers gently through the dirt. When you find a worm, note:
- a wide, light-colored band that surrounds the worm. It's closer to the *front* end than the back.
- hundreds of tiny bristles that help the worm grip. They're hard to see, so feel them by sliding your fingers gently from the back end to the front. Bristles grow only on the worm's *underside*.

Now watch the worm move. Set it down— right side up—and notice how it digs into the soil, headfirst. Psst...don't forget to replace the soil and rock you disturbed. They make homes for many small animals.

Never Say *Die*

Sw-o-o-sh, sw-o-o-sh. Skates on ice. Wayne on skates. After his father flooded the backyard in Brantford, Ontario, Wayne hit the "rink" at 7:00 a.m. every winter day. He skated for more than an hour before school and was back at it by 3:30 p.m. Barely stopping for dinner—he ate in his skates!—he didn't head inside until 9:00 p.m. Sw-o-o-sh.

He played hockey with neighborhood kids, but sometimes his dad set empty soap bottles out on the ice and Wayne worked on his skills alone. He slid his puck between and around them, firing at targets in the net. Again and again. Then he replaced the puck with a harder-to-control tennis ball and took more shots.

When he turned six, Wayne played on a hockey team with bigger kids—10-year-olds—in the Brantford Atom League. Even for his age, he was small. He drowned in the team's sweater and struggled to keep the top end of his stick free of it. But he practiced and practiced, and his hockey got better.

Soon Wayne was playing too well for his own good. At 10, he scored an outstanding 378 goals in 69 games, and many hockey parents became jealous. They booed him and yelled at his family. "I learned that jealousy is the worst disease in life," he later said. But that didn't stop him from playing.

At 14, Wayne was asked to join a team in Toronto, where he would live with the family of one of the players. There was a serious downside—leaving his own family— but he saw it as a way of pursuing his dream of playing in the National Hockey League (NHL).

Suddenly Wayne found himself playing hockey with athletes who were in their twenties. Although he struggled with his small size, he kept up with his teammates, scoring two goals in his first game with them.

By the time Wayne Gretzky turned 17, in 1978, he had signed a contract to play professional hockey, earning a $250,000 bonus, plus $100,000 the first year. Big bucks, especially compared to the $5 an hour he had earned filling potholes the summer before! "The Great One," as he was nicknamed, soon became one of the best hockey players ever.

PERSIST, PERSIST, *Persist*

"Follow through whatever you commit to," Wayne's father told his son. And he did, practicing hockey daily despite his small size...despite the unhappiness that jealousy inflicted...despite the early separation from his family. Wayne's determination to follow through on commitments was a big part of what made his career possible.

Being doggedly persistent is just as important to scientists as it was to Wayne. Their research seldom goes smoothly. They often run short of money or time. They might have trouble locating enough of the bacteria or the type of criminals they need as subjects for their studies. And they might have to be away from home for long stretches, studying pyramids in Egypt or penguins in Antarctica. It's lucky that scientists don't give up easily.

American physicist Albert Einstein figured that achievements in science were mostly a matter of character—the persistence, or *will* to discover. After graduating from university, he couldn't get a job as a researcher, but he didn't let that keep him from the science he loved. When he was hired by a Swiss patent office in 1902, he hid his physics books under his desk. Each day, he sped through his patent work, then pulled out his physics notes and continued developing his theories. He worked relentlessly, trying to figure out solutions to complex puzzles, such as how energy is related to mass. But his persistence paid off. In 1921, he was awarded the Nobel Prize in physics.

You, too, have heaps of persistence. How else would you have learned to ride a bike?

You didn't give up the first time you lost your balance...or the nineteenth or twentieth time, either. You kept trying until you could ride well without thinking about it.

Don't let your tremendous determination flag now. You'll need the power of persistence to succeed at everything you commit to—from singing on stage to running a business or playing pro baseball. Just think of Jackie Robinson. When he put on a Brooklyn Dodgers uniform in 1947, he became the first African American ever to play baseball in the major leagues. He faced years of hostility—even death threats—from players and fans. But he didn't give up. During his remarkable 10-year career, he played ball in six World Series and won the National League Most Valuable Player award in 1949.

> **"Constant dripping hollows out a stone."**
> —Lucretius, philosopher

BRAINPLAY

⭐ Check around your house for examples of persistent forces that change tough material over time. Are there signs of wear in the wood or rug where people step on stairs or walk down hallways? Any erosion of soil, rock, or concrete beneath a water downspout or leaky tap? How are the wheels on the car? What do these signs of change tell you about the power of persistence?

⭐ Persistence can build things up as well as wear them down. For instance, thickened skin, called calluses, are the body's way of protecting itself from frequent rubbing and irritation. Running barefoot can cause calluses that protect the bottoms of your feet from rough ground. Plucking ukulele strings can produce calluses that prevent your fingers from blistering. Think of the things you do, including the games you play, that might cause your skin to thicken. Can you spot any calluses building up?

⭐ From one end of a room, toss each of the playing cards in a deck into a pail on the floor at the other end. Then gather up the cards, and repeat. Keep track of how many times you go through the deck before you can toss at least 10 of the 52 cards into the pail. See how persistence pays off.

The *Great* Roundup

Rocks, stamps, bugs, coins. Charley gathered whatever caught his eye. Collecting was what he did for fun—like playing with his dogs, seeing how fast he could run, or fishing in the river behind his house.

Charley liked to hike, too. During the summer holidays, he and his family often left their home in England to trek around northern Wales. There, he built up his collection of shells and gathered more rocks and bugs.

When he was a teenager, Charley spent time hanging around a natural history museum. The curator taught him about the plants and animals on display and encouraged Charley to keep collecting specimens.

Charley also liked hunting for insects with his buddies. Sometimes, they competed to see who could uncover the most beetles—and the greatest number of species—in the least amount of time. Charley usually won because he used his own special methods for finding beetles. He'd speed-peel hunks of moss and bark off old trees and scoop goo from swamp barges, then search through it all for bugs.

Once, he uncovered three beetles at the same time, but they ran off in different directions. He caught a beetle in each hand, then popped one of them into his mouth to free up a hand for grabbing the third. But the beetle inside his mouth oozed a liquid so bitter that Charley was forced to spit the bug out. Besides being fun, collecting insects taught him how to recognize, compare, and classify different species—even based on their taste!

In 1831, when Charley was 22—and more often called Charles—he got a chance to travel around the world as a naturalist on a survey ship, the HMS *Beagle*. Although he was seasick, he explored every stop on the five-year voyage and collected plenty of plants, animals, fossils, and rocks.

Back home, Charles spent years looking over what he'd gathered on his trip. He was especially surprised at how species taken from each of the Galapagos Islands of the Pacific Ocean differed from every other species. The differences helped him develop his "theory of natural selection" to explain how species evolve.

He figured, for instance, that big-beaked finches could eat more food—big nuts—when meals were scarce than smaller-beaked finches could. So more of the big-beaked finches survived and produced chicks. In turn, these big-beaked chicks produced more big-beaked chicks for generations until that species of finch all had large beaks on the island where big nuts grew. On islands with other kinds of nuts, finches developed different characteristics that helped them survive.

In 1859, Charles (Charley) Darwin published his theory of natural selection. The book stirred up so much excitement that it sold out on the first day! Charles became recognized as one of the greatest naturalists ever.

Collect WHATEVER'S NEAT—AND CLASSIFY IT, TOO

When you think of it, it's amazing that Charles, an *amateur* scientist, made such a huge contribution to science. But he had always been a keen naturalist and an enthusiastic collector. His skills in building and classifying collections—and his passion for nature—helped him gather and study specimens, and form his famous theory.

Collecting and classifying objects and events are what scientists often do—whether they're studying mushrooms, minerals, or murders. Sorting what they gather helps them make and test theories and find solutions to problems. By collecting and classifying feathers taken from airplane engines, American scientist Roxie Laybourne identified the kinds of birds most likely to strike planes and cause crashes. She used that information to reduce bird-plane collisions, suggesting ways to keep certain flocks away from airports.

It's natural to collect what interests you—tropical fish for your tank or postcards for your scrapbook. What you collect today might not fascinate you forever, but keep your love of collecting active. It's a great way to practice classifying—and that's useful whether you become a lawyer gathering and grouping facts for a court case or a mechanic organizing tools and engine parts.

Besides, collecting is a fun way to learn. Former United States president Jimmy Carter still enjoys finding out about the Native people who once occupied his family's farmland in Georgia. "From the time I was five years old [in 1929], my father and I were fascinated by Indian artifacts," he said. "I never walk in a field or along a stream without constantly looking for flint points or pottery fragments."

BRAINPLAY

⭐ Honor a great collector. Every February 12th, celebrate Darwin Day—the birthday of Charles Darwin—by holding a Collector's Gala at your house. Invite your friends to show off their collections and tell each other about them. Find out how people around the world celebrate Darwin Day by visiting the Darwin Day Program Internet site listed on page 117.

⭐ Round up 30 books from around your house. How many ways can you group them? For starters, think of sorting the books by topic or length or cover (hard/soft). See how many different ways of grouping the books your friends can dream up.

⭐ Looking for an idea to start a new collection? How about one of these:
- school badges or pins
- plastic dinosaurs
- feathers
- souvenir hats
- cones from different evergreen trees
- stuffed animals
- flags
- wildlife stamps
- cereal-box prizes
- different kinds of seeds
- soaps in neat shapes and colors
- model cars
- elephant ornaments
- magazines or comics from a particular decade—the '60s, '70s, or '80s

One Fish, Two Fish

Mention New York City and most people picture tall buildings and bustling traffic—not fish. But "most people" doesn't describe Genie. As a little girl in the early 1930s, she was left at a New York aquarium on Saturdays while her mother sold newspapers at the Downtown Athletic Club. Genie's father had died, and her mother was struggling to make a living.

Still, putting in time at the aquarium was no hardship for Genie. Hour after hour, she glued herself to the big glass tanks and watched the fish dart through the water. She noticed how they used their side fins like boat oars to move ahead, stop, back up, and turn. She observed how they breathed, taking water into their mouths and passing it out through their gill slits. And she watched them chase down food and sometimes, scare away other fish.

Genie learned so much from observing the fish tanks that she soon started giving "tours." She offered to take other visitors around the aquarium and show them what she had discovered. Her enthusiasm was infectious.

Then Genie decided that her Saturday visits to the aquarium weren't quite enough. She pleaded for some glass tanks of her own so she could watch fish at home. Although she lived in a tiny apartment, her mother found places to fit in a few tanks. Genie set up her own mini-aquarium so she could see fish every day of the week.

It surprised nobody that Genie studied fish when she grew up and went to college. From there, her work as a marine biologist took her around the world on thousands of undersea dives—some inside submersibles—where she could observe fish in their natural homes.

Eugenie (Genie) Clark became especially interested in one group of fish: sharks. She set up experiments to study their behavior and intelligence. She even taught lemon sharks to hit underwater targets with their noses. When they did, a bell rang, and they were rewarded with food. Soon they linked the ringing itself with the food. Over the years, Genie's work with sharks earned her many honors—and a very special nickname: "Shark Lady."

Observe THE WORLD AROUND YOU

Watching fish as often as Genie did gave her a sense of the animal like nothing else could. Observation is an important investigative tool, and she used it to discover a lot about fish and their behavior. As well, observation proved to be a powerful motivator for Genie. If she had spent Saturdays at the zoo instead of the aquarium, she might have become more interested in monkeys, snakes, or elephants than in fish.

All scientists learn by observing. If something can't be observed someway, somehow, then scientists can't study it. American forensic scientist Skip Palenik uses his observation skills with microscopes to track down criminals. From the time he got his first microscope, at age eight, he was amazed at all he could see in close-up examinations of little things, such as rug strands. Now he studies rug strands clinging to the clothing of a corpse to learn more about the location of a murder.

Of course, observing means more than seeing. It also involves hearing, smelling, touching, and tasting. Scientists use tools—as Skip uses microscopes—to help each of their senses observe more keenly. Stethoscopes, for instance, make it possible for scientists—and doctors—to hear what's happening inside hearts, stomachs, and intestines.

You are an observation machine. Every day you draw on all your senses to take in what's happening and to get around. What senses you use most depends on the situations you're in. When you are cycling to school, you depend largely on sight. When you attend concerts, you focus on hearing. But don't let any of your senses grow dull with disuse. If you're a doctor one day, you'll need most of your powers of observation to diagnose illnesses in your patients. If you're an author, you'll want to make a bustling market come alive for readers by describing the sights, smells, sounds, textures, and tastes you observe.

BRAINPLAY

⭐ World-famous American lecturer Helen Keller (1880–1968) was both blind and deaf. Yet at age five, she knew when her mother was leaving the room by feeling the vibrations her feet made as she crossed the floor.

Have two friends challenge you to use your sense of touch to observe. Sit at the head of a table with your eyes shut, fingers closing your ears, and elbows resting on the tabletop. Invite one friend to sit on the left side of the table and the other, on the right.

Ask your friends to place their palms on the table, then jiggle it slightly for a second at a time. They can nod silently to each other to indicate who should go next—in no particular pattern. Use the sense of touch in your elbows to observe who is making each vibration, then call out the name. See if you can get it right most of the time.

⭐ Take a close-up look at the world through a magnifying glass or plastic magnifying card. Check out objects both inside and outside your house. Can you spot details and colors you've never noticed before?

⭐ Author Mark Twain (his real name was Samuel Clemens) was a superb observer. As a boy in the 1840s, he spent summers at his uncle's Missouri farm where his senses ran riot with "the faint odors of the wildflowers, the sheen of rain-washed foliage, the rattling clatter of drops when the wind shook the trees." He also observed what people did and how they reacted to events such as possum hunting, berry picking, and storytelling. Years later, he used his rich observations from those summers to write his classics, *The Adventures of Huckleberry Finn* and *The Adventures of Tom Sawyer*.

Spend a day making observations—the sights, sounds, smells, tastes, and textures of your world. Use some of those observations to tell a story, as Mark Twain did, or write a poem, compose a song, or paint a picture.

Keeping Track

Ted was lucky. He could visit Forest Park Zoo whenever he wanted. That's where his father worked, and the zoo was just six blocks from home—so close that the family could hear the wolves howling in their pens at night.

Over meals, his father told stories about the bears, monkeys, lions—even the African sheep—that lived in Forest Park. On his days off, he took Ted to the zoo for peeks behind the scenes.

In 1908, when Ted was only four, he began to pack a pad of paper and a pencil along on those trips. He sketched the animals, then filled scraps of wallpaper with his drawings when he got home. Sometimes he drew on the walls in the attic. And he kept paper by his pillow in case he felt like drawing at bedtime. "Ted always had a pencil in hand," his father noticed.

But Ted's sister, Marnie, teased him. She didn't think his drawings looked like anything she had seen in Forest Park Zoo. Many of the animals in Ted's pictures had wildly exaggerated features. One beast that he called "WYNNMPH" sported super-long ears. And his drawings often combined features of different animals—bears with feathers and birds with fur.

Still, Ted wasn't getting his sketches *wrong*. He was recording the animals the way he wanted to remember them. And it's a good thing he did because years later, Ted—whose full name was Theodor Seuss Geisel—found a wonderful use for his drawings of zoo critters. They came alive when he began writing and illustrating books as Dr. Seuss.

Using the name of a street in his hometown of Springfield, Massachusetts, Ted published *And to Think That I Saw It on Mulberry Street* in 1937. It was his first book for young readers, and it told the story of a little boy named Marco who dreamt up wild and crazy ways to "see" a plain old horse and wagon. Remind you of Ted?

He referred to his early zoo sketches for many other books, too. In *If I Ran the Zoo*, Gerald McGrew is a young zookeeper who imports "the strangest odd creatures that ever did walk": elephant-cats, lions with 10 feet, and a hen that roosts on another hen's head.

From *How the Grinch Stole Christmas!* to *The Cat in the Hat*, Ted's books became favorites with children everywhere. Even after he died, NASA named a spacecraft after him: the Data Relay Solar Electric Utility Spacecraft, or DRSEUS. People call it "Dr. Seuss."

Record **SPECIAL OBSERVATIONS**

When Ted visited the animals in his father's zoo, he recorded his impressions with drawings, not words. That's what came naturally to him. And instead of sketching what he actually saw, he outlined what mattered to him—the critters that appeared in his imagination as he watched the animals in the zoo.

Different people have different ways of recording their observations. Many take notes with words or other symbols instead of making sketches like Ted did. Some do both. But most people, including scientists, try to record exactly what they saw, heard, smelled, touched, or tasted.

Keeping records lets scientists compare observations, look for connections, spot patterns, and learn more. Think of Charles Darwin. If he hadn't developed the habit of tracking what he saw and where he found it, he wouldn't have learned all he did from his fantastic, round-the-world collections. Margaret Fountaine (1862–1940) filled sketchbooks with carefully labeled illustrations of caterpillars from many different countries. Along with 200 drawers of the butterflies she gathered, her drawings are a valued part of a museum in England today.

You are a natural record keeper. In the past, you may have kept track of what was in your collection of dolls or train set by making crayon marks in a catalog. Now you might observe each June day before the end of the school year by marking off the days on a calendar. You might also keep a diary of special events in your life or a log of the birds, bugs, or frogs that you've seen.

Keeping track of what's important to you helps you build on past learning and experiences. Recording which diseases, vaccines, and medicines you've had helps you stay healthy. Logging your baseball stats from game to game helps you set goals to improve. Even writing a journal of the bright ideas that pop into your head when you're least expecting them can be invaluable. As brilliant as they are, they can disappear from the back of your busy brain and get lost if you don't jot them down.

> "There are three things I always forget. Names, faces, and— the third I can't remember."
> —Italo Svevo, writer

BRAINPLAY

⭐ When you're making comparisons over time, recording observations helps you keep track of changes. Watch a young plant—even a weed—that's growing outside or in a pot indoors. Check it on the same day each week and write or sketch your observations, such as changes in the number and size of leaves and flowers, and in the height of the plant.

⭐ Early in this book, you read that when astronaut Roberta Bondar was a child, she pretended her neighborhood was another planet. She kept a record of her findings by taking pictures of the "life-forms" she saw. Snapping photos is a way of recording observations. If you have a camera that you can use, keep track of the two-legged or four-legged "life-forms" that visit your house. Put the photos in an album and add labels that name your visitors and say when they came.

⭐ Scientists need YOU to track your sightings of everything from butterflies and moths to loons and whales. Check the Internet for wildlife surveys that you can take part in. As well, do one or both of these:

• Join a Frog Watch team that's collecting data about frogs and toads. In the United States, visit www.frogwatch.org. In Canada, visit www.cnf.ca/frog.

• Take part in annual bird counts. They're often held near the end of December. Ask local birdwatching groups how you can get involved with bird counts in your area.

Walk On!

Heather was only six when her mother nearly lost her leg in a dreadful car accident. After spending months in the hospital, she hobbled around home on crutches. Everything she did took more time and effort than it once had. Heather had never seen her look so tired and sad.

Three years later, her mother left the family. It became Heather's job to buy the groceries, prepare the meals, and do the laundry for her father, brother, and younger sister. She must have felt her life in Britain was very tough—and compared to the lives of many of her friends, it was.

Then it got worse. Her father was sent to prison when she was 13, and Heather had to move in with her mother. Soon she ran away. Poor and often homeless, she eked out a living for several years before finally setting herself up as a model.

As difficult as Heather's life was, she discovered she wasn't alone. In fact, at 22, she came across more misfortune than she had ever experienced. She had been holidaying in eastern Europe when a terrible civil war broke out. Suddenly, she was scrambling to help thousands of people who were seriously injured or homeless. For two years, she worked hard as a model to raise money for them.

In 1993, life clobbered Heather again. Walking across a busy street in London, England, she was hit by a speeding motorcycle and tossed into the air. She lost her left foot at the scene, then doctors had to remove her damaged leg below the knee.

Becoming an amputee herself made Heather even more aware of the needs of others who had been maimed. She learned, for instance, that amputees often replaced their artificial limbs with new ones of different sizes or types. So she set up a way for people to donate replaced limbs to those who desperately needed them.

Today, Heather Mills McCartney continues to raise funds for amputees (partly by modeling again). She also counsels them and shows, by example, that losing a limb or struggling with poverty doesn't need to keep people from achieving whatever they want. And she tries to prevent needless deaths and injuries by asking countries to ban land mines—explosives hidden in the ground during warfare. Long after wars have ended, these mines remain active, blowing up on impact and killing or maiming innocent people, including children. No wonder Heather is highly recognized as a United Nations Association Goodwill Ambassador and has received so many awards for her volunteer work, such as Britain's Gold Award for Outstanding Achievement.

Compare WHAT YOU OBSERVE

Throughout her life, Heather has been learning by comparing observations of people and events. She saw, first-hand, how injuries and poverty affected people, including herself. Comparing her losses with those of others helped her understand their plight and the kinds of support they needed—and put her needs into perspective. By encouraging people to compare their lives to those of amputees and people threatened by land mines, she has raised funds and gained support for banning mines. And by counseling amputees to compare their lives to hers, she has become an inspiration worldwide.

Making comparisons is important to scientific minds. Researchers often examine people, objects, and events and study them in relation to one another. In 1912, German meteorologist Alfred Wegener compared the west coast of Africa to the east coast of South America. He concluded they were so similar that they had likely been connected at one time. Today, North American anthropologist Kathy Reichs compares the size, shape, and condition of unidentified human bones— old and new—so she can reassemble skeletons, individual by individual.

Think of all the comparisons you've made. As you grow older, they become more complex. You might have compared raw carrots with boiled ones, uncovering the changes that cooking made. After playing a few sports, you might have found that you enjoyed baseball more than swimming. And now you might compare your problems with those of a child in Iraq and conclude that your life isn't nearly as tough. With your senses and your mind tuned to comparisons, you'll be better equipped to put observations of all kinds into perspective—and draw wiser conclusions.

> "We cannot know anything about ourselves or the world without making comparisons..."
> —Edith Cobb, sociologist

BRAINPLAY

⭐ Compare the *same* things in *different* ways:

- Examine a rock or a leaf with your eyes alone, then with a magnifying glass or plastic magnifying card. Note the difference in the details you observe.

- Throw a Frisbee, right side up, with its rim curving down. Then throw it upside down, with its rim curving up. Compare how well it flies. Can you see the effect of the rim in making a Frisbee's flight stable?

- Sound travels farther and faster through water than it does through air. At a lake where you can safely swim or wade, ask a friend to stand a short distance away and hit two rocks together underwater. Listen with your ears underwater. Then ask your friend to hit the rocks together above the water. Listen with your ears above the water. Is it easier to hear in the water or the air?

⭐ Compare *different* things in the *same* way:

- Listen to the sounds made by two or three common birds. Compare the patterns of their calls. Check bird guidebooks for clues about what the calls mean.

- Find out which ball has the greatest bounce: a baseball, golf ball, or tennis ball. Stand in front of a long mirror, and drop each ball from shoulder level to a hard floor. Compare the height of the three bounces as seen in the mirror. If you don't have a long mirror, ask a friend to help you observe the height of the bounces. Why do you think the balls were made to bounce differently?

- On three different days of about the same temperature and humidity, compare the time it takes your straight-from-the-shower wet hair to dry completely by:
  - letting it dry on its own,
  - using a towel, and
  - blowing it with a hair dryer.

People of the Forest

Bedtime for Biruté meant stories. Her mother told riveting tales of early Egyptians, Greeks, and Romans. Hooked on ancient history, Biruté read books about other faraway people in long-ago times—Aztec warriors in Mexico and Incan rulers in Peru.

Still, the first book that six-year-old Biruté borrowed from the library had nothing to do with history. *Curious George* was about a monkey who met a jungle explorer wearing a big yellow hat. Along with her parents' love of nature, the book inspired her to explore the outdoors. Biruté spent hours roaming her neighborhood "jungle," a big, treed park in Toronto, Ontario. She crept up on turtles and spied on ducks. "In my imagination, I was exploring untouched wilderness," she recalled.

In high school, Biruté learned about orangutans, intelligent jungle apes with shaggy red-brown hair. She found their humanlike ways fascinating. What's more, she discovered that orangutans—their name means "people of the forest"—are closely related to human beings and that they have lived on Earth even longer than people have. "They must resemble our own ancestors who stood at the beginning of prehistory," she thought.

When she became an adult, Biruté brought together the things she had loved to do: learn about history, explore the outdoors, and study orangutans. For many years, she explored the jungles of Borneo and Sumatra in Southeast Asia (though she didn't wear a big yellow hat). There, she observed the orangutans in their natural homes. The ways of the great apes that she studied provided background to the human history that had always intrigued her. Studying them helped her understand more about human origins and how human nature might have developed.

At work in the jungle, Biruté Galdikas connected her many observations of orangutans. She found a link between their visits to certain trees and the times that those trees produce the most fruit. She connected the number of lessons young orangutans learn with the number of years they spend with their mothers. And she saw how damage to the jungle is related to a fall in the population of orangutans.

Today, Biruté is a world expert on the shaggy red-brown apes. Based on what she's learned from her studies, she's also crusading to keep their homes from disappearing and the orangutans from becoming extinct.

MAKE *Connections*

Biruté linked her interests in history, the outdoors, and orangutans as she grew up and studied apes in the jungles of Southeast Asia. But by bridging her experiences, she

BRAINPLAY

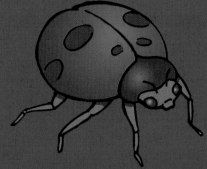

⭐ Practice making connections by becoming an ecosystem detective, someone who checks out everything—living and nonliving—in a particular place. Grab a magnifying glass or plastic magnifying card and examine an ecosystem, such as a small corner of your yard. See some grass, weeds, seeds, flowers, or bushes? How about dirt, pebbles, sticks, fallen leaves, or dewdrops? Any insects, spiders, eggs, worms, slugs, or snails?

Check it day to day and keep track of your observations. Can you spot ways that the growth or actions of one "player" in your ecosystem affect others? For instance, do weeds that grow tall crowd or shade other plants, making it hard for them to survive? As dead leaves gather on the ground, do they smother low-growing plants but provide food and cover for more insects?

⭐ Ladybugs don't eat apple trees, but can you think of a link between them? If you said that ladybugs gobble up aphids that can suck the life out of trees, pat yourself on the head. Now exercise your connecting skills by suggesting an *eating link* between each pair below.
- snakes and lettuce
- bats and wheat
- owls and corn
- people and grass

See what links your friends think up. Their ideas may be different from yours.

enriched more than her own interests. She also contributed years of observation and study to science. The connections she discovered in the world of orangutans help people understand the great apes and their needs.

Being able to make connections is part of being any scientist. In the 1990s, University of California marine biologist Jane Watson examined links between sea otters and the seaweed called kelp. She observed that where otters lived, they gulped down lots of red sea urchins, and the kelp flourished. But where there were no sea otters, the urchins soared in number and ate up most of the kelp. The loss of tall, thick kelp forests also meant the loss of food and

> **"Humans and all of the rest of nature are tied together in a complex but fascinating web."**
> —Laurence Pringle, science writer

⭐ Think about the actions described in the chapters you've read so far:

- let your mind overflow with wonder,
- ask questions—always,
- think for yourself,
- set your imagination soaring,
- investigate: search for facts,
- persist, persist, persist,
- collect whatever's neat—and classify it, too,
- observe the world around you,
- record special observations,
- compare what you observe, and
- make connections.

They link with one another in many ways. For instance, you're more likely to observe and compare the things you wonder about. Can you suggest other links? As you read about other actions in the rest of this book, watch for even more connections.

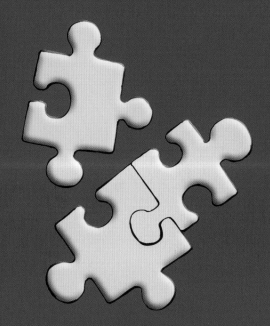

shelter for many fish, sea slugs, and other ocean animals. The connections that Jane studied showed that sea otters play an important role in keeping these ocean communities alive.

You have always made connections. You relate mealtimes to the sounds of someone working in the kitchen. You connect your own lack of sleep with the crankiness you feel the following day. You link dry soil with withering plants and a rising demand for hockey cards with their higher selling price.

Being able to make connections is a skill that helps you understand the relationships between many objects and events—from the links between polluted water and disease to the links between education and income. Understanding relationships helps you make wiser decisions and take stronger action.

Hear the *Harmony*

Louis was a street kid. A tough one. Growing up poor in the early 1900s, he knew he had to be strong just to survive. What he called home in New Orleans, Louisiana, ranged from a shack without water to a cramped apartment in a rundown building. He seldom had clothes other than the ones on his back. Sometimes he didn't even own a pair of shoes. And to find enough to eat, he often had to pick through the garbage.

For Louis, the one wonderful thing in his life was music. It flowed from the doors and windows of the dance halls and bars throughout his neighborhood. Bands paraded through the streets, and musicians blew their trumpets and saxophones along the sidewalks and on the docks. Morning, noon, and night, these sounds filled Louis's head—rich with their patterns of rhythms, melodies, and harmonies.

Louis and his friends tried singing for fun and for the few coins that were tossed their way. They formed quartets that strolled the streets, belting out popular songs of the day. Louis had no training in music, but he listened closely to the others and made up harmonies as he sang.

One New Year's Eve, when Louis was about 12, he got his first big break—but not the way he might have hoped. He had taken a gun belonging to his mother's boyfriend, and when he pulled it out on the street, a police officer spotted him.

Louis spent two nights in jail before he was hauled into court, then sent to a "waifs' home" for troubled and homeless boys. He had lost his freedom, but for the first time, he had a clean place to live and decent food to eat. Best of all, the home had a band, and he had a chance to join it.

After banging out rhythms on a tambourine and a drum, Louis was handed a horn one day. He'd never even held one before, and he couldn't read a note of written music.

But he listened to the pattern of notes the band played and figured out some harmony to add—as he had done when he sang on the streets. Then he pushed the valves on the horn until he heard the notes that matched the harmony in his head.

Louis Armstrong was on his way. He struggled for years to build a career as a professional performer, but eventually he took his place as one of the greatest jazz musicians in the world. For 50 years, he recorded hit songs, composing dozens of them himself. Presidents, kings, and queens were thrilled to hear him sing and play his trumpet. Oh, y-e-a-h!

SPOT *Patterns*

During his hard early life, Louis's ear was well tuned to patterns. He heard them in the melodies, harmonies, and rhythms of the music that surrounded him. And as soon as he got a chance, he used them to make music of his own. Just like British-born pianist George Shearing. In 1922, when George was only three, he strolled up to a piano, used one finger to pick out tunes he knew from the radio, and soon after, started composing.

Scientists take their own natural abilities to recognize patterns and hone them into professional tools for their work. They hunt for patterns in the data they gather, then use them to try to explain things. Patterns of symptoms help identify diseases, and patterns of clouds, wind, air pressure, and humidity help forecast weather.

American physicist Richard Feynman was still a baby when his father encouraged him to play with a stack of floor tiles, placing one white tile after each pair of blue tiles. Soon Richard was producing simple designs on his own. When he grew up, he searched for much more complex patterns among the data in his physics research, winning a 1965 Nobel Prize for his work in the field of quantum electrodynamics.

Mathematics—the language of science—is a search for patterns. That's what a great mathematician discovered when he was a young boy at school in Germany during the 1780s. Carl Gauss's teacher had asked his class to find the sum of the numbers from 1 to 100. All the students settled down to add 1 + 2 + 3 + 4... Except for Carl. He noticed a pattern that saved him loads of time and effort: The biggest number (100) added to the smallest number (1) equaled 101, and so did the next biggest number (99) when added to the next smallest number (2). And on. There were 50 pairs of numbers and they each totaled 101. So Carl simply multiplied 50 by 101 and got the answer (5050) in a jiffy.

Although few people can ever see complex patterns as easily as Carl Gauss did, you are a natural pattern spotter. As an infant, you recognized a pattern of eyes, nose, and mouth as a face—and grinned in response. Now you spot patterns of all kinds, such as daily traffic patterns of rush hours and slow times; and busy streets and quiet ones. Recognizing traffic patterns helps you choose the best time and route to bike to your cousin's place.

When you are grown, the patterns you notice will be useful, too. If you're designing race cars, you might discover patterns of drag reduction, tire angles, and steering mechanisms that make your vehicle the speediest on the track. If you're an investment banker, you'll be watching for patterns in data that flag changes in buying trends. And at home, you'll notice behavior patterns, which will help you understand your family. Watching for patterns is a skill worth hanging onto.

> "Recognizing patterns is like a journey. It's like finding the paths that will allow you to go forward...or that tell you to start over again."
> —Jonas Salk, medical researcher

BRAINPLAY

⭐ Ask your friends to add up the numbers from 1 to 100—just as Carl Gauss's class was asked to do. Point out that they don't have to add the numbers in order. See if anyone uses a pattern to find a shortcut. Then show them the neat pattern that Carl used.

⭐ Watch the body language of members of your family. Under what conditions do they fidget? Clear their throats? Raise their eyebrows? Scratch their heads? Keep track of your observations, then look for patterns, such as fidgeting when they're bored and restless or raising their eyebrows and clearing their throats when they're about to scold. Tell your "subjects" what you noticed, and see if they agree with you.

⭐ Make several different patterns using 30 squares of the same size, 10 in each of three different colors. You might choose to draw the squares on paper with crayons or felt markers, or cut them out of scraps of material. Can you see any small patterns that appear within the larger patterns?

⭐ Clap your hands in different rhythm patterns, such as clap, clap, CLAP, clappity, clap, clap, CLAP. Can your friends repeat each pattern exactly? Have them clap out some patterns for you to imitate.

Pigeon on Horseback

Dreams of soaring the skies flooded Ada's mind as plans for a "flying machine" took shape in her head. And just after her 13th birthday, in 1828, she began to put her wild ideas down on paper. At first, Ada focused on designing a machine that would glide like a bird. She spent months studying the way birds were built, especially their wings. To help with the research, she examined the body of a dead crow she had found in a field.

Then Ada roughed out a design that called for wings made of paper and wire. They would attach to her body at the shoulders. She figured out how big they would need to be—in proportion to a bird's wings—in order to lift her weight. And she set up a "flying room" at her home in England, equipping it with ropes and pulleys for getting the wings into position.

At some point Ada must have lost faith in that design, because she soon moved on to another plan. Perhaps thinking of the strong steeds that pulled carriages in her day, she designed a flying machine shaped like a horse. It called for a steam engine that powered a huge wing on either side. She pictured herself mounting the machine and riding off through the clouds.

As much fun as flying would be, Ada planned a practical use for her machine—delivering letters. With a pouch, map, and compass, she figured she could travel anywhere in the country, moving the mail faster than it had ever been moved before. She was so excited about her plans that she began to sign her name as "Carrier Pigeon."

Ada Lovelace never did take to the skies in a flying machine, but she continued to plan and design things. As a young woman, she became fascinated with an early form of today's computer, called the Analytical Engine. She focused on developing "software applications"—though that term wasn't used in her day—and designed a program for the Analytical Engine to calculate a long, complex series of numbers. More than 100 years before the beginnings of the computer revolution, Ada's work earned her fame as the world's first computer programmer.

Design OR PLAN STUFF

It doesn't matter that Ada's interest in making flying machines didn't produce any. What does matter is that she was exercising her designing skills. She planned what she wanted to do, considered models (bird wings) that worked, adapted what she discovered, then developed a design. As an adult, she used the same basic designing skills and considered math models to come up with a workable program.

Scientists design their projects in similar ways. They learn what they can from other sources, organize their ideas, plan out what they think might work, then test it out. Engineer Marc Brunel, for instance, noticed that a wormlike clam, called a shipworm, scraped through wood with its shells. As it did, it produced a chalky lining that kept the tunnel from collapsing. In 1818, he designed a shield—like a huge shell—that allowed workers to dig a tunnel beneath England's River Thames. As the shield moved ahead, crews lined the tunnel with bricks to prevent the river from breaking through, just as shipworms use chalky secretions to line their tunnels.

When you were still a preschooler, you were designing or planning stuff— naturally. Think back. Perhaps you came up with a plan for an outfit you hoped would give you the powers of Superman: an S on a shirt and a towel for a cape. Or you might have designed a unique train by tying a duck, truck, and other toys in a string behind an "engine"—your tricycle. Maybe you cut a hole out of the side of a cereal box, creating a "screen" that let you watch your own "movies" as you dropped drawings inside.

The ability to plan and design is a skill you would do well to exercise. One day, it might help you lay out a garden, plan a business, organize firefighting teams, or research a cure for cancer. French biologists and filmmakers Claude Nuridsany and Marie Pérennou used their designing skills to make a fantastic movie. *Microcosmos* uncovers the true-life world of little critters—mostly insects, spiders, and slugs. Fifteen years of research and three years of shooting went into making the film, and it took two years to design the special equipment needed—microscopic cameras and super-sensitive microphones. Now that's designing!

BRAINPLAY

⭐ When Russian Igor Sikorsky was 12 years old, he built a model of a helicopter that really flew. Years later, in 1939, he constructed the first full-sized, practical helicopter. He said his best design ideas came from watching hummingbirds fly.

Suppose you wanted to design an emergency rescue machine that could save toddlers who had fallen down deep, narrow wells. If you based your machine's design on an animal, as Igor Sikorsky—and Marc Brunel—did, which animal might you choose? Which features of that animal would be useful to your machine? Just for fun, sketch a design of your emergency rescue machine and give it a snappy name.

⭐ One third-grader came up with a simple design to keep from losing the cap from her tube of toothpaste. She glued one end of a rubber band to the cap and the other end to the tube. Ask members of your family to name a small problem that they experience around the house. Can you design a simple solution?

⭐ Look over this wacky design for a "Woof Walker," an automatic dog walking machine. What problems might it have? How might you improve it?

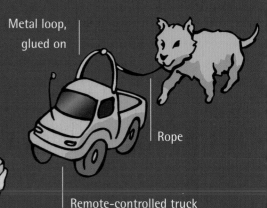

Metal loop, glued on

Rope

Remote-controlled truck

Beating the *Kiss* of Death

Mattie was only 10 when she first started working. She took a job at Amoskeag Mills, a six-story cotton factory in New Hampshire. In 1848, it was common for children in mill towns to work. Besides, Mattie's father had died, and the family was desperate for the income.

Working at the mill wasn't easy. For 13 hours a day, Mattie hauled away big bobbins filled with thread and stuck empty ones in their places. The clatter from more than 600 wood-and-iron looms was overwhelmingly LOUD, and the cotton fuzz that filled the air made it hard to breathe.

Worst of all, danger lurked in the mill. Sharp, steel-tipped shuttles flew back and forth across the looms, drawing long threads to weave cloth. When a thread broke, a shuttle was likely to give a "kiss of death," as workers called it. It would shoot off track and stab whoever was running the loom. These accidental "kisses" had killed children that Mattie knew.

After spending two years at the mill, she became determined to make the work safer. Whenever the weavers took breaks, she checked out the looms, looking closely at how they were threaded and how the shuttles moved.

At home, Mattie jotted down some ideas. She made sketches of the looms, then tried varying the way they operated. When she thought that a few of her ideas might work, she pulled sticks of wood from the family's woodpile and built a small model of a loom. Then she tested her ideas. "Would this make the loom safer...would that...or that?" she wondered.

Weeks passed. Mattie tried idea after idea...making guess after guess. Nothing seemed to help. Finally, she thought of bringing the loom to a dead halt when a thread broke. On her model, she attached a little chunk of wood near a spring by the shuttle.

As the shuttle moved, she deliberately broke its thread, and—YES—the chunk of wood stopped the shuttle, bringing the loom to a standstill! Amoskeag Mills soon added this simple safety feature to all of its looms, and Mattie became a hero.

When she grew up, Margaret (Mattie) Knight invented other things, based on the informed guesses she made. She found a way to make a machine that could cut, fold, and glue paper bags so that they had flat bottoms—like grocery bags. Mattie invented so many things that she earned several nicknames, including Queen of Paper Bags.

TAKE A *Guess*

Think how Mattie's guessing skills saved lives at the cotton mill. First, she learned all she could about the looms and the problem with the shuttles. Then she made a series of informed guesses about how the looms might work more safely and tested each of them.

That's what scientists do, too. Only they call a guess a "hypothesis," and it's not any old guess. It's based on the best information they can gather. Then the researchers design studies—sometimes inventions—to test the hypothesis.

While watching elephants in a zoo, American biologist Katy Payne felt what she called "a faint throbbing in the air." It reminded her of the vibrations she felt in her chest whenever church organists played their lowest notes. She figured that the elephants might also be producing low sounds—so low that they were below the range of human hearing. So she returned to the zoo with a machine that could detect low frequencies. Sure enough, the vibrations were coming from the elephants. Katy guessed that they used them to communicate with other elephants and later tested her hypothesis in Africa by watching the animals respond to one another's rumblings.

Even though you're not a professional scientist, you make informed guesses all the time. You compare the amount of homework you have today with what you had yesterday and estimate the time you need to finish it. Knowing about how far you can leap, you judge whether or not you can jump across a stream. You go to a movie you think you might enjoy, guided by the opinions of friends who've already watched it and your own interest in the movie's storyline.

BRAINPLAY

★ Sometimes you need to make estimates, a form of guessing. Just like other kinds of guessing, it's based on whatever information you can get. The better the info, the more accurate the estimate.

Suppose you were asked how many people attended a spring concert at school. You might come up with your estimate in one of the following ways:

- Knowing how many people the school auditorium can seat, you eyeball the crowd. You figure the auditorium is full, about three-quarters full, half full, or one-quarter full. Whatever fraction you choose, multiply it by the seating capacity of the auditorium.
- Knowing the number of seats per row, you note the number of rows that are roughly full, three-quarters full, half full, and one-quarter full. Multiply each by the number of seats per row and add the four results.

Look over this illustration of concert-goers and estimate the attendance both ways. Here's the info you'll need:

- Seating capacity of the auditorium: 300
- Seats per row: 20

Check how accurate your estimates are by actually counting the people in the illustration.

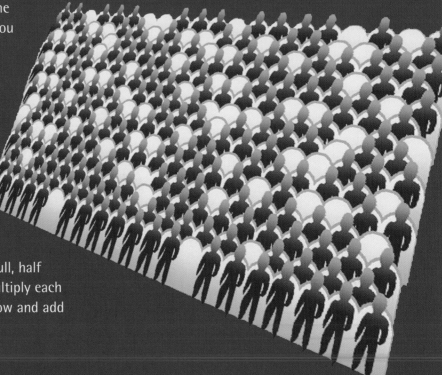

When you're grown, you'll make many more educated guesses. Based on experience and information, you'll decide if your car has enough gas to reach the next town. If you're a doctor, you'll be hoping that your diagnosis—often an informed guess—is correct. If you're a store owner, you'll be banking on which bicycles or books or dishes will sell best. Making educated guesses is an important part of discovery, so keep it up. It's a handy tool to have in your cool kit of science skills.

★ Without really thinking about it, people estimate the weight of objects they're about to lift and adjust the amount of muscle power they figure they'll need. Tease a friend by giving out false clues for an estimate. Put a light object in a big box. Close the box, then lift it—in front of your friend—as if it's very heavy. Hand over the box and see if your friend applies too much muscle power, raising the box high.

★ Flight pioneer Wilbur Wright guessed that if he built gliders so that pilots could twist the wing tips—one up and one down—the gliders might stay level during gusts of wind. He based his guess, or hypothesis, on his observations of turkey vultures tipping their wings in similar ways.

Would the same design feature improve a paper airplane? It seems like a good guess, so try it out. Using diagram "A", build a paper plane. Then have a friend create a "gust of wind" along the flight path of your plane by fanning a slim, hardcover book. Note what happens as you send the plane zooming past the gust of wind.

Diagram "A"

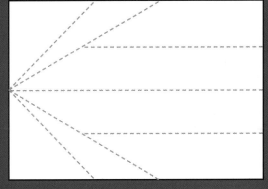

Now bend the wing tips—one up and one down (see diagram "B") and fly the plane past another gust of wind. Does the plane level out? Repeat both kinds of flights several times.

Diagram "B"

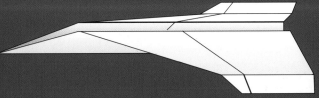

Getting in Touch

Three years old—and blind! Louis had been playing in the workshop where his father made shoes and saddles. The boy was punching holes in scraps of leather with a pointed tool called an awl. One extra hard push had caused it to slip, stabbing him in the left eye. What's worse, the eye became infected, and the infection spread to his right eye. Louis lost his sight completely.

In 1819, at age 10, he left home to attend a school for blind boys in nearby Paris, France. There he found a few books he could read by moving his hands slowly across the pages. The letters of each word had been raised.

Still, those books weren't easy to read. Like other students at the school, Louis had a hard time feeling the difference between letters that were alike, such as "h" and "n." Besides, the books were huge and heavy. One of them weighed 180 kilograms (400 pounds)! The school had to split it into several volumes.

Louis tried to think of ways to make reading easier and faster for the blind. He searched for a simple code with symbols that would stand for the letters of the alphabet. He even considered borrowing symbols from mathematics or foreign languages.

When he couldn't find anything that worked well, Louis tried inventing his own codes, then tested them. But they didn't work, either. Too confusing...or too bulky...or too hard to learn...or too complex to remember.

One day, Louis heard about "night writing," designed by Captain Charles Barbier of the French army. The captain had invented a way to read messages in the dark by feeling groups of up to 12 raised dots representing different sounds.

That gave Louis an idea. He created a code that was similar—but used symbols that were simpler and smaller. And by the time he was 15, he had designed a system of patterns—each with up to 6 raised dots—that stood for letters, sounds, and some words. As well, he was able to use his code to write by making dots with a pointed instrument called a stylus.

Over the years, Louis Braille's special code has made it possible for blind people everywhere to read and write quickly and easily. Named "Braille," the code was soon adapted to most of the major languages.

Make Mistakes THEY'RE SO REVEALING

It's easy for people to assume that Louis Braille enjoyed instant success in creating a system of reading for the blind. You now know otherwise. Louis failed over and over again in his attempts to find something that worked well. Luckily for everybody, he persisted until he hit on a good system. The scientist in him knew that making mistakes is just part of the process.

> "The only real mistake is the one from which we learn nothing."
> —John Powell, geologist and explorer

Scientists expect to be wrong—again and again. Finding what doesn't work is a method of discovery. It narrows down the possibilities, making it easier to learn what does work. "Science progresses by correcting its mistakes," says zoologist Richard Dawkins.

Take *Tyrannosaurus rex,* a gigantic dinosaur that stood on two strong legs, snapping up prey with its powerful jaws. For years, many scientists figured it could run as fast as 72 kilometers (45 miles) per hour. Recently, John Hutchinson at Stanford University, California, set up computer models to calculate the leg muscle that a *T. rex* would need to support its huge body while running. He concluded that the dinosaur wasn't speedy at all. His best "guesstimate" was that *T. rex* would not have traveled a quarter as fast as scientists had believed. Human sprinters could have escaped its jaws, so scientists have been changing their ideas of how *T. rex* hunted and ate.

But...perhaps John Hutchinson made a mistake, too. One day, scientists may find that—unlike modern animals—*T. rex* had some special mechanism that allowed it to move fast while supporting an incredible mass. If so, science will correct itself again.

Sometimes, mistakes even lead to great discoveries. In 1928, British scientist Alexander Fleming made the mistake of leaving a sample of disease-causing bacteria uncovered, and mold contaminated the sample. To his surprise, Alexander saw that the mold prevented the bacteria from growing. His discovery led to the making of a life-saving drug called penicillin.

Your life so far has been riddled with errors. Good thing. You must be making progress! Like everybody else, sometimes you might confuse words that sound alike, such as "commuter" and "communicator." Assembling a kite, you might insert the supporting rods the wrong way, making it hard—or impossible—to fly it. Or preparing for a hike with friends, you might confuse kilograms with pounds and pack along just 1 kilogram (2 pounds) of food, instead of 2 kilograms (4 pounds). Oops! But you learn from your mistakes.

> **"Anyone who has never made a mistake has never tried anything new."**
> —Albert Einstein, physicist

Don't stop now. Keep on learning even though you trip up occasionally. Being bold enough to make errors helps you tackle new challenges. And when you're an adult, that will make you a better skier, parent, gardener, musician, dentist, or welder. It might even help you come up with a new discovery. After all, self-stick, removable Post-it notes are the result of someone's failed efforts to produce a strong glue.

BRAINPLAY

⭐ With your best buddy, develop a secret code. Choose a symbol to stand for each letter of the alphabet. For example, % might stand for "a," and 7 for "b." Try writing each other short messages—as fast as possible. You're bound to make mistakes, but keep rolling. You'll learn to write in code through practice, and the mistakes you make will be useful in identifying the symbols that need more attention.

⭐ Suppose you goofed and made a jug of lemonade that was too weak to enjoy as a drink. Can you think of a different—but useful—way to use it up? (Clue: think "freeze.") What if your parents tried making jam, but it didn't thicken. Can you suggest a delicious alternative use?

⭐ Solve a problem through "trial and error." Ask a parent to give you several keys that open things in and around your house. Work through the keys, trying them in different locks until you see what each one opens. You'll discover that finding what doesn't work narrows down the possibilities and makes it easier to learn what does work.

Easy Does It

Few people take hammers and chisels for a stroll along the seashore. But Mary's family did. They lived in Lyme Regis on England's southern shore during the early 1800s. The town had once been a port for smugglers, and much earlier, a home for many prehistoric creatures.

When Mary's father wasn't working as a cabinetmaker, he took the family hunting for fossils, the remains of ancient life inside rocks. He showed them what to look for and taught them how to remove the fossils—carefully, patiently—-from ocean cliffs at low tide. To earn extra money, the family sold these fossils to summer visitors who vacationed in Lyme Regis.

When Mary was just 11, her father died, and the family was plunged into poverty. Older brother Joseph found a job, but it paid poorly, so Mary quit school to spend more time finding fossils to sell. She often went searching alone. Sometimes she had to wade through icy water to check the cliffs. There were occasional mudslides and tumbling rocks. Fossil-hunting could be dangerous work. It also took loads of time and patience. Months could pass before Mary even found another fossil. Then she might spend several weeks removing and cleaning it, and several more trying to identify it.

One day, when Joseph was passing the cliffs, he spotted some unusual bones. Neither he nor Mary had seen anything like them. "Were they the remains of an ancient crocodile?" she wondered.

For a whole year, she tried to find other parts of the strange fossil creature. Then one night, a raging storm made her job a lot easier. The wild winds and rains that lashed the cliffs exposed the rest of the beast's skeleton. It was more than 4.5 meters (15 feet) long—much too big for Mary to remove on her own. She gathered a few of the townspeople together and showed them how to help her with the careful, painstaking job.

As word of Mary's discovery spread, scientists thronged to Lyme Regis to see it. And what a discovery it was! Mary had found the first complete skeleton of a "fish lizard," an ichthyosaur, left from the age of dinosaurs.

Still, because she was poor—and female—Mary Anning was unable to get any schooling in science or any formal training in finding fossils. Instead, she studied on her own, gradually gaining knowledge and skills that impressed professional scientists. As an adult, she found other important fossils, such as a plesiosaur, a sea serpent, and a pterodactyl, a flying reptile. Today, many of Mary's fossils are displayed in museums around the world.

HANG IN THERE *Be Patient*

It may seem impossible to be patient and excited at the same time. But it's not. If Mary and her helpers had failed to exercise patience during the thrilling uncovering of her "fish lizard," they might have flung bones from the cliff—breaking or losing some in the process. As a lifetime fossil hunter, Mary's patience was invaluable at every stage: tracking down the remains, retrieving them, and identifying what they were.

"You get the chicken by hatching the egg—not by smashing it."
—Arnold Glasow, humorist

All sciences call for patient work. At research stations in Australia and parts of Asia, biologist Naomi Pierce has been studying the relationships between caterpillars and ants for more than 15 years. Some of the caterpillars ooze food for the ants, which, in turn, protect the caterpillars from life-threatening dangers, such as being invaded by parasites. Naomi discovered that the caterpillars "talk" to the ants through vibrations, but discovering just what the different vibrations mean will take more years of patient work.

You've already displayed plenty of patience. The fact that you are reading this book right now demonstrates patient effort on your part. Just think—you learned the letters of the alphabet and what sounds they make. You learned to grasp the meanings of those letters when they're strung together in words and when the words are combined in sentences. Now you demonstrate patience every time you read a gripping mystery without first flipping to the back of the book to see how it ends.

Patience is something you'll always use. Working with your powers of persistence, patience makes it possible for you to practice and develop the skills you need for everything from driving a car and playing chess to teaching school and raising a family. So be smart: be patient.

BRAINPLAY

⭐ Try hunting for fossils on cutbanks along roads. Check with a museum or library first to learn the best areas to search and ask to look at any fossils—or their photos—that have been found locally.

Hunt only where it's safe and legal, and collect only fossils that are loose. Unless you're a trained collector, hammering or chiseling for fossils can hurt both you and the environment.

If you find a fossil, wrap it carefully in newspaper. Note where and when you found it. Then rinse it off gently at home. Return to the museum or library for help identifying it.

⭐ For centuries, people have played a card game called Patience, or Solitaire. Napoleon Bonaparte, once emperor of France, played Patience to pass time when he was exiled to the island of St. Helena in 1816. Now there are more than 1,000 variations of the game. Try one of them—Clock Patience—but be warned: it takes plenty of patience and luck to win.

Object of the game: to turn up all the cards from aces to queens before the four kings appear.

1. Deal a deck of cards in piles of four—set out like the numbers around a clock. See the illustration.
2. Put the 13th pile in the center of the "clock," and turn up the top card in that pile.
3. Place that card beside its corresponding "hour" pile around the clock (2 by the

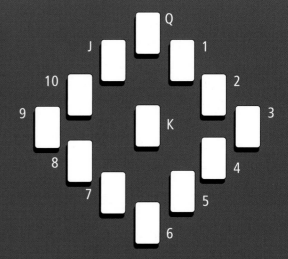

"second hour" pile, 7 by the seven o'clock, and so on). Note that aces are used as the number 1, jacks are 11, queens are 12, and kings are 13—in the center.

4. Take the top card of each pile that you place a card beside and put the new card by its corresponding "hour" pile.
5. Continue playing until each pile contains all four cards of its number.
6. The game ends when you turn up the fourth king.

⭐ Talk about patience. Wildlife photographers must have a bundle. Some spend hours waist-deep in ponds or perched high up in trees to get the shots they want. Taking a close-up photo of a trilling toad, North American photographer Tim Fitzharris notes, "I had to practically lie down in the same soggy puddle with the toad."

Try your hand at bird photography. When you spot birds going to and from a tree, hide behind a nearby bush or fence and focus your camera on a branch. Wait patiently for a bird to land right there. Snap!

Mother Goose Makes *Good*

Toddlers often hear stories of Mother Goose, but who ever tries to BE a mother goose? Thomas Alva, nicknamed Al, that's who. He was the kind of kid who rarely accepted anybody's word. When his mother told him that a goose sat on eggs, keeping them warm until they hatched, he had to see for himself.

One day, he disappeared into a barn where his family found him curled up on a nest of straw that held goose eggs. The two-year-old said he was trying to make "little gooses" come out. And he might have done it if he'd been allowed to stay there long enough.

That experiment was only the first of thousands that Al did. At six, he tried to figure out how fire burned—the kind of fire he saw in the lamps that brightened his Ohio home in 1853. Inside the family barn, he piled up dry sticks and lit them, but what happened next was more than he ever imagined. The whole barn caught on fire, and Al had to run for his life!

The following year, the family moved to Michigan, and soon Al's mother let him set up a basement lab to test the experiments he read about in books. But he also liked to dream up his own experiments. For a while, he was interested in flight—a passion that was hard on his friends. He had watched people use gas to raise hot-air balloons, so he convinced his pal, Michael, to swallow heaping amounts of Seidlitz powder—bellyache medicine normally used in small doses. When the powder dissolved in water, it produced loads of carbon dioxide. But all that gas did nothing to make Michael rise. It just made him sick—though not as sick as another chum who took part in a different failed experiment. Al had reasoned that birds flew because they ate worms, so he fed that friend a thick drink of smushed worms and water!

When he was 16, Tom—the name that Al preferred to be called by then—started working as a telegraph operator. On the quiet night shift, he received few messages, which gave him plenty of free time. Still, his manager insisted he send a signal every hour to prove he was awake. "What a nuisance!" Tom must have thought, so he set up a clock to hit a switch that triggered the telegraph to relay a signal automatically.

By 1869, Thomas (Tom) Alva (Al) Edison began devoting all his time to inventing. Before long, he was coming up with inventions that changed the world: the light bulb, the phonograph, the electric train, and the storage battery that made cars possible. During his lifetime, he registered an amazing 1,093 patents!

Experiment SEE FOR YOURSELF

Some of Tom's experiments—using gas or worms to achieve flight—made his friends sick. Other experiments, such as starting a fire inside a barn, were downright dangerous. No one encourages that kind of research, but Tom's efforts to find out things for himself deserve respect. He wasn't content to accept what others believed. His determination to experiment helped him become one of the most remarkable inventors the world has ever known.

Scientists are ready experimenters, too. French entomologist Jean Henri Fabre experimented with pine processionary caterpillars that follow one another very closely, each one producing a silk thread that the next one walks on. The leader is whichever caterpillar happens to be first. Jean wanted to see if the caterpillars would stay in their procession even if they weren't getting anywhere.

BRAINPLAY

⭐ You've heard that water evaporates (changes from liquid to vapor), but see for yourself. Set out half a glass of water where it won't be touched. Then check it daily and count the number of days that pass until all the water has evaporated, leaving the glass dry.

⭐ Here's something else you can see for yourself. Pour several scoops of pond water into a pail. Check for a backswimmer, a common water bug. Put it—and some of the water—into a clear jar and pour back the rest.

One day, a parade of caterpillars passing through his garden completely circled the rim of a large pot. Jean quickly swept away the silk path that led up the pot—plus all the remaining caterpillars that were still climbing. The caterpillars left on the rim then formed an unbroken chain that continued to circle the pot, producing an ever thickening silk trail.

Finally, they followed a caterpillar that stumbled over the rim and accidentally began a path downward. But Jean could scarcely believe his own observations: despite cold, hunger, and fatigue, the pine processionary caterpillars had been on the rim of the pot for seven days. He figured that, although they rested about half that time, they had walked for 84 hours. Traveling at a rate of 9 centimeters (3 1/2 inches) per minute, they had circled the 135 centimeters (53 inches) around the rim about 335 times!

You do experiments, too. Perhaps you try out different shampoos to find one that controls your fly-about hair. Maybe you stick a birdfeeder in an oak tree, then in a hawthorn, to see which attracts the most birds. Take a leaf from Tom Edison's book: keep on experimenting—you'll be glad you did.

One day, you might find a way to streamline security checks for airline passengers or invent robots that keep gardens free of weeds. Your experimenting nature could even land you a dream job, like Christy Sumner's did. As a special-effects technician for moviemakers in Hollywood, California, she experiments almost every day, figuring out how to make cars flip over, mirrors fall down, or fires flare up—all "mysteriously" and right on cue.

Notice the backswimmer swims upside down—on its back. It's colored the opposite way to most animals, which are darker on their backs. Holding its pale back away from the sunlight makes the backswimmer harder for predators to spot.

Experiment to see if a backswimmer can—and will—swim on its front. Take your clear jar into a dark closet and shine a flashlight up through the bottom. Does the backswimmer flip, turning its darker underside toward the light? Return the insect to its natural home when you have finished.

★ Experiment with two ways of building walls. Using Lego bricks, make one wall by snapping the bricks together on top of one another—straight up in rows (see "Wall A"). Make the second wall by overlapping the bricks (see "Wall B"). Why is the second wall better than the first wall?

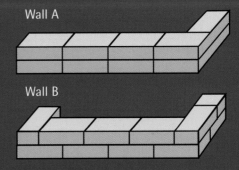

Wall A

Wall B

The *Pulse* of a Wrangler

Teenage Galileo had a lot in common with today's teens. He liked to laugh, play music, daydream, and figure things out for himself. He also liked to argue. In fact, when 17-year-old Galileo entered the University of Pisa, Italy, in 1581, he argued so much he was nicknamed *Il Attaccabrighe,* The Wrangler. One of his biggest arguments was about the best way to prove ideas. He figured that scientists should experiment—not just ponder ideas, as the ancient Greeks had done for years.

One day, Galileo was daydreaming in the university cathedral when he noticed a big brass lamp hanging by a chain from the ceiling. The lamp was swinging back and forth, back and forth. What fascinated him was that each swing seemed to take the same amount of time—no matter how far or how little it swung.

To make sure he wasn't imagining things, Galileo measured the time each swing took, using the beat of his own pulse. Even if he'd had a clock handy, in those days there was nothing more accurate than a pulse for measuring short periods of time.

Back in his room, Galileo decided to test and measure what he had seen. He attached different weights to strings of different lengths, then set them swinging. He used his pulse to time the swings. Just like the swaying of the cathedral lamp, the long and short swings of any one string took the same amount of time. He noticed that the amount of weight he attached didn't change the time the swings took—but the length of the strings did.

Over his lifetime, Galileo Galilei made significant discoveries by experimenting and measuring. Not surprisingly, he came up with a "pulse counter," which helped doctors check heartbeats. He developed the telescope into a useful scientific instrument that helped support the theory that Earth revolved around the Sun.

He also showed that more than reasoning was needed to discover what happens when objects fall. Ancient Greek philosopher Aristotle wrongly thought that heavy objects fall faster than light ones. But Galileo and others demonstrated that that wasn't so. His measured approach opened new doors to science.

Measure STUFF

Although they lived in different times and places, Galileo had a lot in common with inventor Tom Edison, described in the previous chapter. They were both great experimenters, people who insisted on discovering things for themselves. And as you can tell, especially from Galileo's story, measuring is important to many experiments.

Of course, there's a place for guessing and estimating in science, too (see "Beating the Kiss of Death"), but scientists can't base precise conclusions on rough figures. Think of the exact measurements that must go into designing and launching a spaceship, for instance. And imagine how exactly chemists must measure what they combine in their labs. It's not enough to mix a *pinch* of this with a *smidgeon* of that.

Biologists have even measured the slight hearing difference an owl experiences in order to find prey in the dark. The bird aims its attacks according to the tiny difference in time a sound takes to reach the left ear and the right ear. That can amount to just 200 microseconds (millionths of a second)!

You've nearly always been a measurer, and you still are. You read thermometers that measure temperatures—inside and out. You mix measured amounts of flour, sugar, baking powder, and other ingredients to make a cake, and you set a timer to track the time to bake it. At the piano, you start a metronome to keep your playing to set speeds. And at track and field events, you click on a stopwatch to pinpoint running times—in hundredths of a second. In the years ahead, paying attention to measurements will be just as important to you, whether you're a big rig driver watching your truck's gas consumption or a politician checking the popularity polls at election times.

BRAINPLAY

⭐ Sometimes seeing is NOT believing. Measuring is. Look at the drawing below. Which line is longer—the line that forms the mouth of the "Goofy Graduate" or the line that forms the bottom of his hat (where it meets his hair)? Measure them both to find the answer. The other lines drawn around them can trick the eye.

⭐ Try Galileo's experiments for yourself. Run a string about 40 centimeters (16 inches) long through the loop of a closed padlock—or something of a similar weight. Ask a friend to hold the string ends together and set the padlock swinging. Use your pulse to time the length of the swings. (Find it by placing the fingertips of your right hand on the inside of your left wrist, just below your thumb.) Or use the second hand on a clock to time the swings. Do the long and short swings of the padlock take the same amount of time?

Repeat the experiment by replacing the padlock with items of different weights, such as a slotted spoon or a spool of thread. Do

the long and short swings still take the same amount of time?

Now use a string half as long as the first one. Swing any one of the weights. Does it move faster than it did on the longer string? Do the results of your experiments agree with Galileo's findings?

⭐ When an astronaut on the Moon dropped a hammer and a feather together, they hit the surface at the same time. There was no air on the Moon to push up against the feather, delaying its fall. On Earth, air can interfere with falling objects. See what happens by doing an experiment:

On a windless day, hold a small board in one hand and a piece of paper the size of the board in the other. Stand by an open window. Ask a friend with a stopwatch to stand below the window—but out of harm's way—to measure how much longer the paper takes to reach the ground than the board does. As you holler, "Here goes!" drop both objects at once. Your friend will start the stopwatch when the board lands and stop it when the paper does.

Repeat the experiment, but first, set the paper on top of the board (no part should hang over), then drop them together. This time, they should land at the same time because the air's upward force on the paper isn't greater than it is on the board.

You can try this measuring experiment with other items of different weights, such as a magazine and a marshmallow or a cereal box and a ball of cotton.

Compute *This*

"You're too young to learn math," said Blaise's father—who was also the boy's teacher—and he locked away every math book in the house. That made Blaise all the more determined to learn. Secretly, he struggled to figure out math on his own. By the time he was 12, he had discovered, independently, that the angles in any triangle add up to 180 degrees. So surprised was his father that he finally agreed to teach the boy math.

In turn, Blaise sometimes assisted his father, a tax collector in 17th-century France. He worked long hours, poring over accounts, night after night. Blaise found their method of using stones to add and subtract so tiring—and boring—that it was easy to make mistakes. He was inspired to search for a better system.

At age 19, after many failures, Blaise invented a mechanical calculator. Called the Pascaline, it was about the size of a shoebox and could sit easily on a desk. The surface was made of metal with small windows where the answers appeared.

Using wheels along the bottom of the Pascaline, Blaise entered the numbers to be calculated, turning gears inside. They rotated like the gears do in a car's odometer—which adds up the number of kilometers or miles traveled.

The Pascaline worked best for adding because the gears turned in only one direction. But Blaise adapted the machine so it could also subtract. It multiplied through repeated additions and divided through repeated subtractions.

For the times, Pascalines were very impressive. They were accurate and quite fast. Blaise built 50 of them, but they didn't sell well. The machines were expensive, especially compared to the cost of cheap labor. And workers, afraid of losing their jobs to the machines, pressured their bosses not to buy them.

Still, Blaise Pascal became well-recognized for inventing his state-of-the-art calculating machine. Today, he's often called the "father of the computer age." Even a 20th-century computer language, Pascal, was named in his honor.

Figure Out ANSWERS

Math intrigued Blaise so much that he rebelled against his father's wishes and started to teach it to himself. But what began as a fascination became something very practical when he turned his mind to developing his amazing Pascalines.

Scientists in all fields depend on math to help them in their research. It's especially useful in exploring relationships between whatever they're studying. England's Florence Nightingale was one of the first to demonstrate that math can even be used to study behavior, such as the way hospital staff cared for patients. While working as

a nurse in the Crimean War (1854–1856) in Europe, she collected and analyzed data about how injured soldiers were treated. Her calculations showed that the number of preventable deaths among the soldiers was related to the low levels of sanitation in the hospital. The results spurred improvements in both military and city hospitals.

Just as a professional scientist is part mathematician, so is your inborn scientist. You easily spot patterns—the key to doing math (remember Carl Gauss in "Hear the Harmony"). And the language you speak shows you have a basic feeling for math. When you talk about what's usual, normal, standard, or ordinary, you demonstrate your sense of what's average (arithmetical average is a total divided by the number of figures that make it). When you refer to what's rare, strange, odd, or extreme, you show your sense of how far things can vary from the average.

As well, you've discovered that you don't need to check every leaf on a tree to be able to describe or draw one. You can pick out a leaf's main features by looking at a sample of leaves, just as scientists and mathematicians study a sample—a part of the group being studied—to figure out information about the whole group.

Even if you don't grow up to be a scientist, architect, computer programmer, or accountant, your life will still involve math. In one way or another, it is part of almost every activity—even mountain climbing. Team leaders, such as Joe Murphy who led a climb up the tallest peak in China, carefully calculate the weight their crew can pack, the energy they'll burn, and the amount of all kinds of food they'll need. They have to figure in the effects of the altitude and slope of their climb, as well as the number of weeks they'll be gone. Their lives depend on math!

BRAINPLAY

⭐ People use math every time they use money, estimating sales taxes and restaurant tips and counting their change after buying something. No wonder the math they're most comfortable with is "money math." Try your own skills at money math by playing a game of Coupon Challenge. Here's how:

1. With a friend, gather 10 coupons from coupon books, magazines, newspapers, or flyers, choosing a variety of values. Shuffle them together in a pile and place it face down.

2. Have your friend turn over the coupons, one by one, while you add up the values out loud. Your friend adds them, too—but silently—turning the coupons as fast as he/she can add them. Your friend hollers "Challenge!" any time he/she reaches a different sum than you do—or flips to the next coupon before you've come up with a sum. Then he/she announces what the sum should be at that point.

3. Check the addition of the coupons played. Whoever stated the last correct sum wins the round and scores a point. If you're both wrong, no one gets a point.

4. Shuffle the coupons and begin the next round. This time, you turn the coupons and add them in your head while your friend adds out loud. The winner is the first to score 5 points.

Game variation: Start with $20 and subtract the value of each coupon. Score the same way you did when you were adding the values.

⭐ Rev up your math skills while riding in a car. Each time you pass another vehicle, add the digits on the license plate. It's not hard, but the practice will make you lightning fast at adding in your head!

⭐ Surprise your aunt by figuring out her age and birth month. Have her secretly write down the digit(s) representing her birth month (10 if it's October), then have her double that number (20). Now ask her to add 8 (28), multiply the answer by 50 (1,400), add on her age (if it's 34, that would make 1,434), then subtract 400 (1,034). Have her announce the final result (1,034). The last two digits (34) tell you her age. The first two digits (10) tell you her birth month—October. The first digit alone would tell you the birth month if the final result had just three digits.

Can you figure out what's happening? The calculations you ask your aunt to do in adding 8 times 50 (400) to her age, then subtracting the 400 later, are only busywork to hide the fact that she is actually giving away her age. By doubling the digits of her birth month, then multiplying by 50, she is really multiplying by 100 (2 x 50). That makes sure that the birth month digits are the first one or two of the final number, that is, they go in the 100s slot. Of course, this trick would work with anyone of any age.

Ha,ha,Ha

Right from the start, life was harsh for Marie. She was born in Warsaw, Poland, in 1867, a time when it was very hard to be Polish. Russia controlled her country, and the Czar was eager to wipe out the language and the ways of the Polish people.

Marie suffered personal tragedies, too. At age nine, she lost a sister to typhoid. When she was 11, her mother died of tuberculosis. Although Marie graduated from high school when she was only 15—and at the top of her class!—she was barred from entering any universities in Poland. They weren't open to women.

With all she endured, it's hard to imagine Marie finding anything to laugh about. But she did. Her keen mind couldn't help but see the humor in inconsistencies—in things or events that don't agree or go together. That's why she enjoyed playing practical jokes as a teenager. One holiday, Marie and her sister Helena planned some pranks on Jan, their host's brother. He was a young man with a big appetite, and he drank a jug of milk with every dinner. Marie and Helena secretly added water to his jug—more each day—to thin the milk. They must have wondered when he would ever notice. Finally, Jan complained that the milk didn't seem to have much color or taste, but he laughed with Marie and Helena when he learned what they had done.

Another time, the sisters asked Jan to do some shopping for them. While he was gone, Marie and Helena "rearranged" his room, which he had always kept as neat as a pin. They strung all his furniture—bed, chair, table, and washbasin—from the ceiling. They even stuck weeds and flowers in his shoes, which they also hung up. Then the girls hid to watch Jan open the door.

Years later, Marie had a chance to study science at a university in Paris, France. There, physicist Henri Becquerel reported a mystery: rocks containing uranium were giving off rays, even when kept in the dark! Other rocks he had tested emitted rays only after being exposed to sunlight or X-rays. The inconsistency fascinated Marie Sklodowska Curie, and she set to work, investigating the uranium rays for years. Her research led to the discovery of radioactivity and her first Nobel prize, in 1903.

SEE THE *Inconsistencies*

Marie was quick to spot inconsistencies. She based her pranks on them, secretly changing the milk that Jan knew well and "rearranging" the room he kept in perfect order. And as a scientist, she worked to explain how uranium rocks, unlike the others that Becquerel tested, emitted their own strong rays.

Seeing inconsistencies is how Italian scientist Luigi Galvani discovered that electricity causes muscles to move. In 1786, he was preserving a dead frog to show his students and hung it with a copper hook on an iron railing to dry. Suddenly, the frog's legs twitched and jerked—an action definitely inconsistent with death! The observation focused Luigi's studies on electricity in the body and also caught the interest of Italian scientist Alessandro Volta. He found that electric currents flowed through the frog's muscles because they brought two different metals, copper and iron, into contact. From this discovery, Alessandro developed the first electric battery, made with two different metals.

Like scientists, professional comedians also make good use of inconsistencies. American funnyman Groucho Marx joked, "One morning, I shot an elephant in my pyjamas. How he got into my pyjamas I'll never know." He phrased his first sentence to sound as if the elephant was the one wearing pyjamas—something that's definitely inconsistent with what elephants do. And Florida humorist Dave Barry wrote, "Everyone is entitled to an opinion. It just happens that yours is wrong." People laugh because his second statement doesn't agree with his first.

"Incongruity is the mainspring of laughter."
—Max Beerbohm, cartoonist

While comedians adopt inconsistencies in many of their jokes, scientists try to weed them out—to explain them. That's what spurred Luigi Galvani and Alessandro Volta to examine electricity, and that's why scientists today try to discover why certain diets help some people lose weight and not others.

But scientists and mathematicians, like humorists, value conciseness—both

BRAINPLAY

⭐ Plan a practical joke on your family. Get a large black-and-white photocopy of a family photo. It can include grandparents, aunts, uncles, and cousins. Stick it on your fridge with magnets. Each day—when no one's looking—use a pencil to change one detail that's inconsistent with the person being changed. For instance, if your brother never wears a tie, draw one on him. If your aunt doesn't need glasses, give her a pair. Does it take your family several days to notice that the photo is changing? Do they find your changes funny?

⭐ Describe the inconsistency that makes each of the following jokes funny:
- Putting peanut shells under my bed keeps bears away. It must work. No bears ever crawl under my bed.
- The night guard at a warehouse spotted a figure in a dim hallway. He fired his gun, shattering his own reflection in a mirror. "But I beat him to the draw," he told his boss the next day.
- Sam and Jane saw two slices of cake on the table. Sam helped himself first, taking the bigger slice. "Bad manners," muttered Jane. "If I'd had first choice, I'd have taken the smaller slice."

  "Well, that's the slice you have," said Sam. "So we should both be happy."

equations and jokes are best when they're brief. And delivering jokes is like writing equations. The steps or parts of each have to be in the right order. As well, humor and math both use expressions and definitions exactly. Mathematician John Allen Paulos says that's one of the reasons people laugh at someone who reads the library sign, "Lower Your Voice," then speaks close to the floor.

You've enjoyed the humor of inconsistencies for years. Besides riddles and jokes, the sight of your sister tripping over her own feet might strike you as funny. It's an unexpected action—inconsistent with the way she normally walks. Even less obvious inconsistencies—noticing a tough teenage boy blush when girls are around—might make you chuckle. So exercise your funny bone. It not only makes you laugh, it helps you spot inconsistencies. And think of the ways that will be useful when you're grown. It might even help you find errors when your checkbook disagrees with the bank's records. And if you ever become a detective, it can help you spot holes in a suspect's alibi!

⭐ Many words have more than one meaning. You can make up jokes—cartoons or riddles—by using these words in ways that are inconsistent with the meaning you intend. You might sketch two robbers handing a woman's slip to a police officer as they dash off, and add the caption: The robbers got away by giving a police officer the **slip**. Or you could turn the joke into a riddle by asking: How did the robbers use underwear to escape? Answer: They gave a police officer the **slip**.

Here are a few words that have at least two meanings each. Try making cartoons or riddles by using them in funny (inconsistent) ways:

- bank: place receiving and lending money OR edge of a river
- horn: musical instrument OR headgear on cattle and buffalo
- mouse: little rodent OR computer equipment
- pop: soft drink OR a name to call dad
- trunk: chest for clothes OR long nose of an elephant

Using a Fine-Tooth Comb

"I used to write picture letters to a little invalid boy years and years ago...Peter was written to him in a letter," said Beatrix. Her "Peter" was none other than Peter Rabbit, the most famous character in the books she wrote and illustrated for children. Along with Flopsy, Mopsy, and Cottontail, he first appeared in 1893 in the pen-and-ink drawings she created as a young adult. But Peter and friends had begun to take shape in her mind much earlier—when Beatrix was a small girl.

She had always loved animals. With her brother, Bertram, she collected all kinds. From Britain's woods and valleys—and pet stores, too—the children sneaked insects, lizards, snakes, frogs, newts, jays, owls, kestrels, bats, rats, and rabbits into their little home "zoo."

Besides taming the rabbits—which hopped around the nursery or curled up in front of the fireplace—they examined beetles and caterpillars under microscopes to see how their body parts were connected. They observed how a bat hung upside down in the parrot cage and how it caught insects. In the notes Beatrix was forever making, she wrote, "I had no idea bats were so active on their legs...and their tail is very useful in trapping flies."

When Beatrix and Bertram found dead animals, such as mice, birds, and foxes, they removed their hides and boiled the flesh off the bones. When the bones were dry, the children fitted them together—reassembling the skeletons to figure out how the animals were built.

Beatrix and Bertram sketched or painted everything they studied. They filled homemade books with pictures of eggs, flower petals, leaves, and toadstools, as well as animals—including drawings of their bones. Even when Beatrix was only 10, her pictures were detailed and realistic. But for fun, she sometimes drew scarves on newts and had rabbits wear bright jackets and hold umbrellas.

As she grew up, Beatrix became interested in fungi. She gathered different kinds, dissected them, and drew precise illustrations. She figured that plantlike growths called lichens were really two organisms—fungi and algae—living as one. And she was right! But the scientists of the day paid little attention to her.

If Beatrix Potter had had the chance to become a scientist, she probably would have. Instead, she used her analysis of animals, plants, and lichens to help her paint pictures. All the time she had spent observing and figuring out how things were put together became invaluable to her work. The books she produced, such as *The Tale of Peter Rabbit*, made her famous.

Analyze BREAK THINGS DOWN

Beatrix observed, collected, compared, and recorded whatever fascinated her. But she also did something else. She analyzed. Like a scientist, she studied animal behavior, examined the body parts of insects, took apart and reassembled skeletons, and dissected lichens. Then she applied her natural analytic skills to her artwork.

Scientists analyze all sorts of things. They break them down into their parts and study their nature. They examine the functions of the parts and look at the relationships between them.

In science, analysis often removes the mystery from things. Spanish explorers in the 1600s saw bouncing rubber balls in South and Central America and thought they must be some form of magic. But a later analysis of rubber balls—produced from the milky sap (latex) of tropical trees—showed that they are made up of long molecules all tangled together. When a ball is dropped on a hard surface, the molecules stretch for a moment before motion inside of them returns the molecules to their original shape. A lot of the energy of the ball's downward motion then becomes upward motion as the molecules return to that shape.

> "Aristotle could have avoided the mistake of thinking that women have fewer teeth than men by the simple device of asking Mrs. Aristotle to keep her mouth open while he counted."
>
> —Bertrand Russell, philosopher

California astronomer Jill Tarter is trying to use analysis to solve mysteries from outer space. She helped found the SETI (Search for Extraterrestrial Intelligence) Institute, which examines sound waves, searching for any radio signals that might have been beamed from other planets. A gigantic radio telescope in Puerto Rico gathers much of the data that the institute looks at. One day, SETI scientists might use their analysis to locate other intelligent life in the universe. If you want to help them, visit the SETI Internet site listed on page 117 and find out how.

You've been a busy analyzer since you were a baby. Sitting in a highchair, you probably squished grapes or blueberries between your fingers, eager to see—and feel—what was inside. Now you might remove the batteries from the TV remote control and discover that it doesn't work if you reinstall the batteries facing the same direction. All part of analysis.

In the years ahead, you'll use your analytic skills even more. A toaster that isn't toasting might have you searching for the part that's not doing its job. Or loose spending habits might have you seeing where your money is going so you can find ways to save more. By building your skills in breaking things down, you'll be better equipped to pinpoint your problems—then solve them.

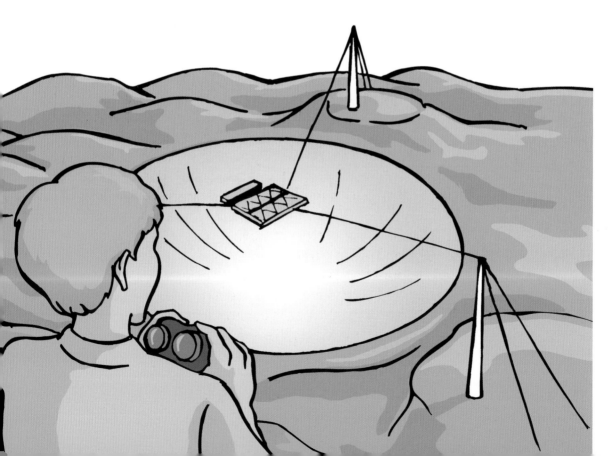

BRAINPLAY

⭐ Analyze the structure of a small object—a ballpoint pen, a toy car, a watch or clock that doesn't work any more—by taking it apart and putting it together again. Don't forget to ask for permission first.

⭐ Break down a picture on your color TV to see what it's made of. Examine the screen closely with a magnifying glass or a plastic magnifying card. Can you see a mass of little rectangles—green, red, and blue lights? Are some of the rectangles brighter than others?

    Now stand back and look at the screen as you normally would. Your eyes—and your brain—mix the bright and dim rectangles of the three shades together, producing the wide range of colors you detect in a picture.

⭐ Analyze dandelion flowers at three different stages:

1. Pick a yellow dandelion bloom. Break it in half—lengthwise— and look closely with a magnifying glass or a plastic magnifying card. The bloom is made up of many little flowers growing side by side, the smallest ones in the middle.

2. Pick a dandelion bloom that has closed up and dried out. Break it open. Find the tiny, green seeds inside—they're sitting beneath the small flowers.

3. Pick a dandelion bloom once it has formed a fluffy white ball. Carefully break into one and notice that the seeds have turned brown. Feel them—they're hard and sharp. Use your magnifier to spot the hooks that seeds use to take hold of soil. Blow the white, hairlike parachutes attached to the seeds and watch them take off.

Tell the World

Golda knew what it was like to be poor. In Russia, she had shared a single room in a stuffy apartment with her mother and two sisters. When they moved to Milwaukee, Wisconsin, to join her father in 1906, their little suite had two rooms and a tiny kitchenette, but no bathroom.

Going to school in Milwaukee was free, but every student had to pay to use the textbooks. Although the cost was small, Golda discovered it was too much for many of the children in her class. When she was only in grade 4, she decided to do something about it: tell everyone. She planned to hold a public meeting and explain the problem.

Working with a friend, Golda gathered together a group of girls from school. She convinced them to help her paint posters to advertise the meeting, making it clear why people should come. The girls also made up invitations and sent them out.

Dozens of people turned up at the meeting. As head of the girls' group—they called themselves the "American Young Sisters Society"—Golda spoke and presented the facts of the problem:

- All students needed to use textbooks in school.
- Everyone was charged to use the books.
- Many students were too poor to pay the charges.
- The society needed to raise funds to cover the charges.

As a result of the girls' efforts, people were willing to donate money to the society!

Golda went on to make many more speeches during her lifelong career as a politician. As she had done in grade 4, she gathered her facts, presented them clearly, and made her point. In 1969, Golda Meir was elected prime minister of Israel.

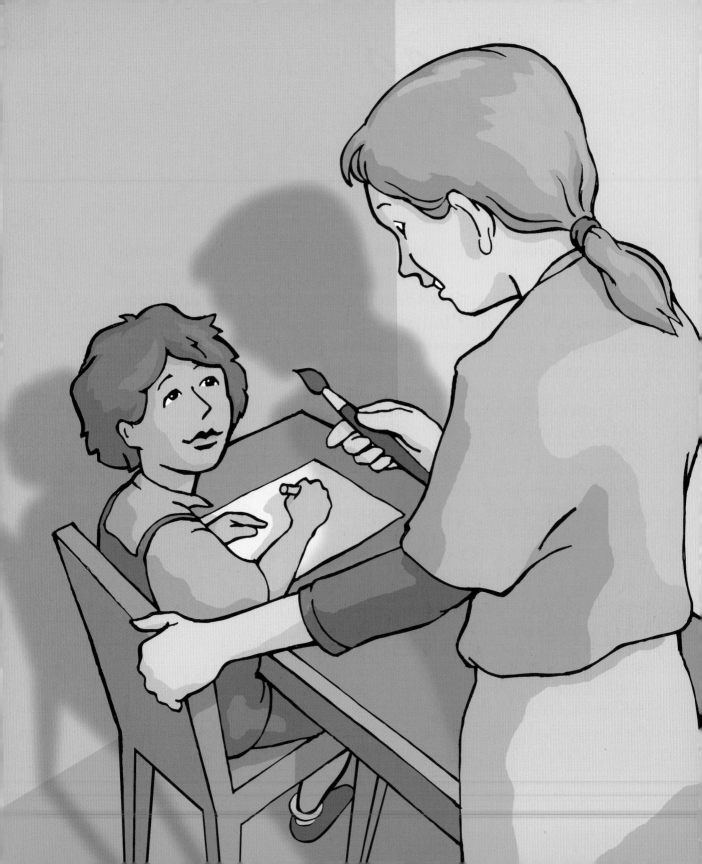

One day, she returned to the Milwaukee school she had attended as a child. The students were still poor and had few opportunities, but they welcomed Prime Minister Meir warmly. Then she spoke to them, sharing something she had discovered: "It isn't really important to decide...what you want to become when you grow up. It is much more important to decide on the *way* you want to live. If you are going to be honest...if you are going to get involved with causes which are good for others...that is sufficient." As always, when Golda had something to say, she said it.

SHARE YOUR DISCOVERIES *Communicate*

When young Golda found out that the textbook charges were too high for students in her class, she explained the problem at a public meeting. For her, communication was a tool for educating others and bringing about change, and she used it well her whole life.

It's just as important for scientists to communicate. Like Golda, they know it's critical to gather the facts and present them logically to others. Information becomes more valuable when it is shared. Then other scientists can add their insights or knowledge, which helps ideas grow.

When scientists report what they studied, how they studied it, and what they found, other researchers can repeat the effort. If those researchers get similar results, they support the findings of the first study. If they don't, the scientists re-examine their work. Communication is the key to cross-checking results. For example, after scientists first linked cigarette smoking with lung cancer and published the results, studies from many different researchers tested the link in their own studies—and discovered the same relationship. Their work led to a widespread anti-smoking campaign.

Scientists often share their findings with the rest of the world—not just with each other. American botanist Margaret Lowman, who studies treetop levels of rainforests, promotes conservation by telling the public what she's doing. In one study, she found that koalas in Australia were innocent of killing off huge

> **"Many ideas grow better when transplanted into another mind than in the one where they sprang up."**
> —Oliver Wendell Holmes, Jr., judge

numbers of the eucalyptus trees they live in. She discovered that ranching practices had caused a beetle boom. The insects were attacking the trees, which were already weak from drought and loss of soil—and that was information ranchers and the rest of the public needed to know.

Ever since you learned to talk, you've been eager to communicate. Now you do more than talk. You share your ideas, observations, and discoveries through e-mails, letters, and school reports. You make drawings or take photos to show what you've found and what's important to you. Everybody benefits by communicating—a patient discussing symptoms with a nurse, an electrician sketching plans for wiring a house, and a company president writing a report for investors. So keep "talking."

BRAINPLAY

⭐ Share your scientific discoveries with your family and friends by telling them (1) what you did, (2) how you did it, and (3) what you found when you tried one or two of these "Brainplays":
  - Find out how a skateboarder does an ollie (see "Tracking It Down").
  - Count the days it takes for a glass of water to evaporate (see "Mother Goose Makes Good").
  - Become an ecosystem detective (see "People of the Forest").

⭐ Instead of telling others about one or two of the Brainplays above, exercise your ability to communicate through pictures. Sketch (1) what you did, (2) how you did it, and (3) what you found. Use a comic strip style, if you like.

⭐ Invite three friends to play a cross-checking game with you—in two teams of two. Ask another person to set out 30 objects (a wide variety), then give both teams a minute to look at them.

Have the teams go to separate rooms where they can write down all the objects they remember seeing. The two players on each team can cross-check their observations by discussing them with each other.

After 10 minutes, have your helper call everyone back. Each team scores one point for every object correctly listed, but subtracts two points for listing any object that was not there.

Did sharing observations help your team's list grow? Did it eliminate any listed objects that weren't actually there? Find out how cross-checking helped the other team get things right.

Windmill of the Mind

"Hmm...would it really work?" Isaac wondered. The toy windmill he had built sat idly on the table in his room. At age 12, he'd been sent to live with the Clarks—a druggist and his wife—while he went to school. In spare hours, Isaac often helped Mr. Clark mix chemicals for the medicines sold in the drugstore, but he liked to build wooden models, too. And Mr. Clark was happy to encourage Isaac, lending him saws, hammers, or whatever else he needed.

The model Isaac had created this time was a miniature of a real windmill he had seen being built that very year—1654. Once the model was finished, there was only one way to see if it worked. Isaac scrambled onto the roof of the Clarks' house and set it up. From there, the windmill could harness the power of the wind. And it did! It even managed to grind up the few kernels of corn he had set inside it.

To operate the windmill on calm days, Isaac had a backup plan. He stuck a mouse, which he called the "miller," inside the model to provide power by running on a treadmill. But of course, the mouse also ate up the corn. The thought of a miller devouring its own ground corn made Isaac laugh.

The thing with Isaac was that he didn't just think a thought, he tested it. He was always experimenting, and he tried hard to get his models—windmills, water-powered clocks, waterwheels, sundials—to work. No one's sure what he had in mind when he attached lanterns to the tails of the kites he made. But as the strange lights danced across the night sky, startling the country folks of England, Isaac must have been testing something.

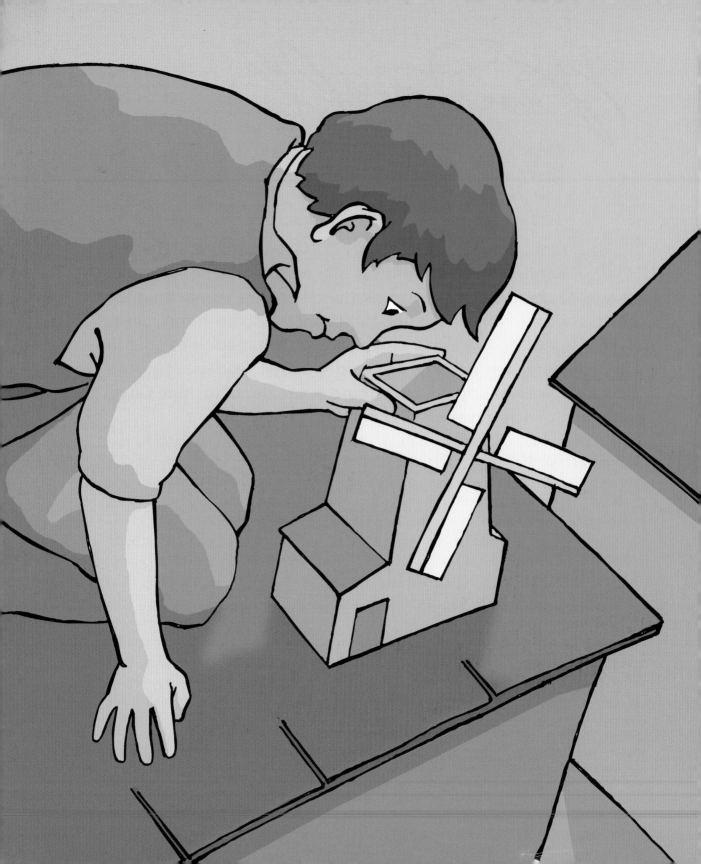

When he grew up, Isaac Newton didn't stop experimenting. In fact, he made that his life, becoming one of the greatest scientists ever. He gave the world the laws of motion, which explain the way things move, and the theory of gravity, which applies as much to planets traveling through outer space as it does to apples falling from a tree.

Perhaps Isaac's biggest gift to the world was the "scientific method." He insisted on testing informed guesses—hypotheses—to answer questions in carefully controlled ways. Before him, Galileo Galilei also saw the value of experimenting instead of depending solely on logic, but Isaac went further. He stressed that experimenting was the key, that no idea was worth anything unless it could be proven by testing, then analyzing the results.

USE THE *Scientific Method*

Isaac's experimenting ways as a boy helped him discover the value of doing scientific experiments when he was grown. Whenever he had a serious question, he found out what he could about it and guessed at what the answer might be. Then he planned an experiment to test his guess and examined the results.

Today, scientists everywhere use the process that Isaac Newton did—the scientific method. After investigating the facts, they build hypotheses and design experiments that often involve collecting data, making and comparing observations, finding connections, spotting patterns, taking measurements, and figuring things out.

Scientists analyze the results, usually with the help of math. They check those results by retesting the hypotheses several times, then report their findings for cross-checking by other scientists.

Consider American scientist Jonas Salk. Using the scientific method, he produced the first vaccine to prevent polio, a virus-caused disease that can result in paralysis—even death.

Investigating the polio virus, Salk learned that there was not just one type, but three. He figured that a successful vaccine would need to spur people's immune systems into producing antibodies that would fight them all.

Jonas Salk tested an experimental vaccine on volunteers, including his family and himself. Everyone produced the needed antibodies. In 1954, the vaccine was retested—on masses of people in North America. The results were amazing. The Salk vaccine went into wide use, and the number of polio cases plunged.

"Millions say the apple fell, but Newton was the one to ask why."
—Bernard M. Baruch, statesman

All of the actions described in this book relate to the scientific method. Many of them, such as asking questions, guessing, experimenting, and analyzing, are key parts of the method. Others, such as thinking independently, imagining, persisting, daring to make mistakes, and being patient, support the method. So it won't surprise you to learn that the scientist inside you has already been using the scientific method.

Although each of these actions enters into the method, you can simplify your thinking about it by reducing it to three basic steps: **G**uess, **E**xperiment, **D**iscovery—**GED** it! Get it? Sure you do. You've already been using these steps without realizing it.

If you thought that substituting ice for cold water made Jell-O set faster (Guess), you probably compared the two ways of making Jell-O (Experiment) and saw for yourself which was faster (Discovery). If you figured most of the neighborhood kids—not just you—wanted a skateboard park (Guess), you might have asked every kid on your block plus a few surrounding blocks (Experiment), and calculated the percentage who agreed with you (Discovery).

In the 1800s, English biologist Thomas Huxley wrote, "There is no more difference between the mental operations of a man of science and of an ordinary person, as there is between the operations...of a baker weighing out his goods...and the operations of a chemist performing a difficult analysis." His point was this: everybody is a scientist—something you've already found out—and everybody uses some form of the scientific method. Remember that, and keep your inner scientist busy.

BRAINPLAY

⭐ You're getting dressed on a hot summer day, and you wonder which T-shirt to wear: black or white. You think you've felt warmer when you've worn the black one, but you're not convinced.

Test out the hypothesis that black holds the heat more than white. Experiment by laying two thermometers, reading the same temperature, in bright sunshine. Cover one with your black T-shirt; the other, with your white one. A half-hour later, compare the temperatures on the thermometers. Check your experiment by repeating it.

⭐ You accidentally spill a whole can of nails into a wading pool in your backyard. You've used a magnet to pick up nails before, but can it work its "magic" in water? You think it can (Guess)—at least, you hope so. But before you borrow a heavy-duty magnet from your neighbor, you want to see if it will work. Drop a few nails into a bowl of water and lower a small magnet into the bowl (Experiment). What happens? (Discovery).

⭐ You or someone you know is sure to have Clue, the classic "whodunit" game. It's been around for more than 50 years. You use a simple form of the scientific method to discover which of the six characters in the game murdered "Mr. Boddy," plus how and where. Based on the cards you are dealt and any information you find out from other players during the game, make a suggestion (Guess) about the identity of the killer, the murder weapon, and the murder scene. Test your suggestion by asking other players if they have any of the cards you named (Experiment). Make note of what they respond (Discovery) and use that to help you form the next suggestion (Guess), test it out (Experiment), and so on, until you can make a final accusation (Discovery).

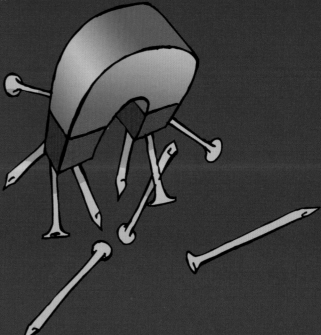

Winding *Up*

Throughout this book, you have been exploring the scientist in YOU—that thrilling part of your inner self that has been with you since day one. It's what makes you the exciting, curious person that you are—ever keen to:

- let your mind overflow with wonder,
- ask questions—always,
- think for yourself,
- set your imagination soaring,
- investigate: search for facts,
- persist, persist, persist,
- collect whatever's neat—and classify it, too,
- observe the world around you,
- record special observations,
- compare what you observe,
- make connections,
- spot patterns,
- design or plan stuff,
- take a guess,
- make mistakes (they're so revealing!),
- hang in there—be patient,
- experiment: see for yourself,
- measure stuff,
- figure out answers,
- see the inconsistencies,
- analyze—break things down,
- share your discoveries: communicate, and
- use the scientific method.

As you were reading about each of these scientific actions, you no doubt discovered how closely related they all are. You found that observing is part of comparing and connecting. Asking questions overlaps with investigating. Designing is linked with experimenting. And so on.

You also probably noticed that, although the story of the featured person in each chapter focused on one action, that person's inner scientist was working in other ways, too. The story of biologist Rachel Carson centered on her investigative skills, but it also told of her ability to wonder, observe, compare, make connections, communicate, and think for herself. The inventor of the Braille code, Louis Braille, was an example of someone who wasn't afraid to make mistakes and learn from them. But his story also demonstrated imagination, patience, persistence, and the ability to spot patterns, guess, experiment, and communicate. Scientific thinking integrates all these actions.

Inside THE RAINBOW

Unlike the people described in this book, some folks lose contact with the scientist inside, or they decide that scientific thinking is used only by professional scientists. Sadly, they ignore or shut out that electrifying part of themselves. They may feel that it's no longer cool to be imaginative or questioning. Or they might believe that scientific thinking takes the beauty or romance out of life.

English poet John Keats (1795–1821) accused Isaac Newton of robbing the rainbow of its poetry by explaining it as white light split into colors. But present-day British zoologist Richard Dawkins defended all scientific thinking when he wrote, "Mysteries don't lose their poetry because they are solved. Quite the contrary. The solution often turns out to be more beautiful than the puzzle."

Don't worry. You won't ever lose contact with your inner scientist—not if you value your scientific self and use it to help you do whatever you choose to do with your life. The best part is that you don't need to change to exercise the scientist in you. Just keep on doing what comes naturally: let your mind overflow with wonder...set your imagination soaring...ask questions...think for yourself...investigate.... You know the rest.

While you're at it, spread your scientific enthusiasm around. Invite others to share your discoveries. Encourage your friends and family to find—and free—the scientists in themselves.

And although you can always appreciate the beauty and "poetry" of a rainbow, it's important to look *inside* it, too—to discover just what light is made of. After all, scientific thinking is the real pot of gold!

Fun Resources for Further Exploration

BOOKS AND MAGAZINES

Burton, Valerie. *Making Photographs*. Toronto: Burgher Books, 1995.

Garden, Nancy. *The Kids' Code and Cipher Book*. Hamden: Linnet Books, 1991.

George, Jean Craighead. Any of her ecological mysteries, such as *The Missing 'Gator of Gumbo Limbo*, New York: HarperCollins Publishers, 1992 and *Who Really Killed Cock Robin?* New York: HarperCollins Publishers, 1991.

Haines, Gail Kay. *Micromysteries: Stories of Scientific Detection*. New York: G.P. Putnam's Sons, 1988.

Highfield, Roger. *The Science of Harry Potter: How Magic Really Works*. New York: Viking, 2002.

Hoff, Syd. *The Young Cartoonist: The ABC's of Cartooning*. New York: Stravon Educational Press, 1987.

Jones, Charlotte Foltz. *Mistakes That Worked*. New York: Delacorte Press, 1991.

Kramer, Stephen P. *How to Think Like a Scientist: Answering Questions by the Scientific Method*. New York: T.Y. Crowell, 1987.

McDonald, Bob. *The Quirks & Quarks Question Book: 101 Answers to Listeners' Questions*. Toronto: McClelland & Stewart, 2002.

Marzollo, Jean. *Superkids: Creative Learning Activities for Children 5–15*. New York: Harper & Row, 1981.

National Geographic Kids (10 issues per year).

Parker, Steve and Jane. *Collecting Fossils: Hold Prehistory in the Palm of Your Hand*. New York: Sterling Publishing Co., 1997.

Simon, Seymour. *The Optical Illusion Book*. New York: William Morrow & Co., 1984.

Taylor, Barbara. *Be an Inventor*. San Diego: Harcourt Brace Jovanovich, Publishers, 1987.

Terban, Marvin. *Funny You Should Ask: How to Make up Jokes and Riddles with Wordplay*. New York: Clarion Books, 1992.

Tumanov, Vladimir. *Jayden's Rescue*. Toronto: Scholastic Canada, 2002.

Wilber, Jessica. *The Absolutely True, Positively Awesome Book about...ME!!!* Minneapolis: Free Spirit Publishing, 1999.

Wolke, Robert L. *What Einstein Didn't Know: Scientific Answers to Everyday Questions*. New York: Dell, 1997.

Wolke, Robert L. *What Einstein Told His Barber: More Scientific Answers to Everyday Questions*. New York: Dell, 2000.

YES Mag: Canada's Science Magazine for Kids (6 issues per year).

VIDEOS

Nuridsany, Claude and Pérennou, Marie. *Microcosmos*. Alliance Video, 1998 (1 hour, 17 minutes).

Nye, Bill, The Science Guy. *Measurements* and *Patterns*. Disney Educational Productions (broadcast version), 1998 (26 minutes each).

INTERNET SITES

Addresses of Internet sites can change often. If you have trouble finding a site, check with a librarian for current listings.

Darwin Day Program	http://www.darwinday.org
Discovery Kids	http://www.discoverykids.com
Inquiring Minds	http://www.inquiringminds.org/bookshelves
National Geographic for Kids	http://www.nationalgeographic.com/kids
Quirks & Quarks	http://www.radio.cbc.ca/programs/quirks
SETI@home	http://setiathome.berkeley.edu
Why Files	http://www.whyfiles.org
Wonderville	http://www.saf.ab.ca
YES Mag	http://www.yesmag.ca

Index

About the Author and Illustrator

Diane Swanson has turned loose her inner scientist in more than 60 factual books for kids, including the multiple award-winning *Nibbling on Einstein's Brain*. Diane's enthusiasm for the world around us and her engaging way with words help prove that there is a scientist in absolutely everybody.

Warren Clark has explored the world as a graphic designer on three continents. His clever, playful style demonstrates his love for illustrations that make you laugh and make you think. *Turn It Loose* is his second book with Diane Swanson.